"Richard Van Yperen master[...] is woven into a divine tapest[...] our journey of faith and connection—both with God and those around us. His devotional is transformative as it beautifully nurtures discipleship between parents and children, mentors and mentees, and small groups seeking deeper spiritual growth."

—Dr. Darren Petersen
School Administrator/College Professor

"Above All Else… is an excellent daily devotional. Through poignant remembrances from his own youth, the author does a wonderful job of bridging the gap between fathers and their children, making this devotional accessible and enjoyable for multiple generations."

—Peter Young
Author of the Amazon best seller Stop The Tall Man, Save The Tiger

"This work by Richard Van Yperen is full of rich biblical truth delivered in a way that constantly points to every participant's need for the grace of our Lord Jesus and the power and presence of his Holy Spirit as we live our lives. The format is accessible and will assist parents in speaking truths that are 'Above all Else' in matter of importance for their teens, while developing good habits of seeking the Lord's wisdom each day. I look forward to growing together with my sons as we walk through this study together. If you take the time to walk through this study with someone else, I believe the Lord will use it in your life as He is doing in mine."

—Tim Barton
Lead Pastor of The Vine Community Church

"*Above All Else* is a compelling continuation of Van Yperen's wisdom series in fresh and engaging form. His trademark storytelling introduces each essential while his skillful questioning draw the reader deeper. *Above All Else* is a quick read by design, but its challenges linger long after you put down the pages. Whether for personal study or group discipleship, Van Yperen is a trusted guide who will take you on a journey of formation."

—Andrew Culp
Executive Director of The Anvil Academy

ABOVE ALL ELSE...

15 KINGDOM OF GOD BIBLICAL ESSENTIALS FOR LIVING WISELY A DEVOTIONAL GUIDE

RICHARD VAN YPEREN

WESTBOW
PRESS®
A DIVISION OF THOMAS NELSON
& ZONDERVAN

WestBow Press books may be ordered through booksellers or by contacting:

WestBow Press
A Division of Thomas Nelson & Zondervan
1663 Liberty Drive
Bloomington, IN 47403
www.westbowpress.com
844-714-3454

Holy Bible, New International Version®, NIV® Copyright ©1973, 1978, 1984,
2011 by Biblica, Inc.® Used by permission. All rights reserved worldwide.

ISBN: 979-8-3850-3658-5 (sc)
ISBN: 979-8-3850-3659-2 (e)

Library of Congress Control Number: 2024922103

Print information available on the last page.

WestBow Press rev. date: 11/11/2024

Dedication
Above all else, this devotional guide is for my children and
grandchildren. My earnest prayer is that they will "Above
all else" daily seek God's kingdom and His will.

CONTENTS

My son, pay attention to what I say;
Listen closely to my words.
Do not let them out of your sight,
Keep them within your heart;
For they are life to those who find them
And health to a man's whole body,
Above all else, guard your heart,
For it is the wellspring of life.
Proverbs 4:20-23 (NIV)

INTRODUCTION

The origin of this daily devotional guide comes from several sources over a period of thirty-four years.

During the school year of 1997 - 1998, I served as an English teacher and a dorm parent for 28 senior boys at the Rift Valley Academy in Kijabe, Kenya. Each week I facilitated dorm devotions in our living room. At the end of the third trimester, I gave each graduate a bound booklet of the devotions for that school year. On the first page, I wrote my last words to these young men ending with the following: *"It is my prayer that you will continue to grow in 'knowledge and depth of insight, so that you may be able to discern what is best and may be pure and blameless until the day of Christ.' (Philippians 1:9-10) As you face the rest of your life, I, along with [the Apostle] Paul, desire for you to 'conduct yourself in a manner worthy of the gospel of Christ.'" (Philippians 1:27)*

Ten years later, when we returned after serving at RVA for four years, I accepted an offer to be the Elementary Principal at Eastern Christian School in New Jersey. During that first year, I invited a former colleague to meet regularly on Friday mornings of the school year. That invitation sparked his invitation for other men to join us. The group grew to 14 men, all of them educators and coaches in the area. First we read Rick Warren's book, THE PURPOSE DRIVEN LIFE, which launched us into studying the Bible. Over a seven years span we discussed what it looked like to live wisely and biblically. At the end of that time, we studied Proverbs 1-9, The Gospel of John 1-4, and James' letter to believers. We named our group, with a bit of tongue in cheek, WISE GUYS. Eventually, I graduated these men encouraging them to make disciples within their spheres of influence. Then, when I retired from serving at Eastern Christian School, I decided to write a book based on our studies over the years. I published

A COMPLETE GUIDE TO GODLY WISDOM in 2019 and then SO WHAT WISDOM in 2021. Presently, each year there is a new cohort of Wise Guys who meet to study Godly wisdom and then graduate as official Wise Guys.

Currently, I am honored to meet with four high school boys for a Bible study Monday mornings during the school year. Two of the boys are my grandsons who asked me to facilitate the study. Then they invited two other boys to join the study. My time with these high school boys has led to this writing project during the summer of 2024.

In addition to the group of four young men this 2024 – 2025 school year, my hope is that the 15 weekly devotions will be primarily used for mutual sharpening. So, my intention in writing this book is for two or more people to enter into the 15 weeks study by meeting once a week, and during the rest of the week each person would daily reflect on the main theme in Day 1. Then in the next meeting, they would share their answers and thoughts from each of the daily reflection devotions, followed by reading the next Day 1 devotion for 15 weeks.

ABOUT THE TITLE AND SUBTITLE

The leading phrase "Above all else" shines a spotlight on a kingdom of God biblical essential. In Proverbs 4:20 - 23, Solomon's instructions for his son highlights the importance of paying attention, listening, and remembering his instructions because they will enhance his son's health and well-being. And then Solomon wrote "Above all else, guard your heart..." (Proverbs 4:23) spotlighting the essential theme needed to activate his instructions. Like any great teacher Solomon focuses on his main idea – "guard your heart" – by likening that to guarding your source of clean water from pollution. (See Week 1, Day 1)

The subtitle - 15 Kingdom of God Biblical Essentials For Living Wisely - takes its cue from Luke 17:20 - 21:

> "Once having been asked by the Pharisees when the kingdom of God would come, Jesus replied, 'The kingdom of God does not come with your careful observation, nor will people say, 'Here it is, or 'There it is,' because the kingdom of God is within you."

ABOUT THE FORMAT

This devotional format is designed to identify and explore a weekly "Above all" kingdom of God biblical essential theme over the span of several days. Each week will start " Day 1" with the words "Above all" or "Above all else" with the primary passage bible verse[s], sometimes quoting directly from the scripture passage, but always seeking to spotlight and apply a main theme or idea. The primary devotional is followed each day by daily reflections designed to develop and anchor further the "Above all" primary theme. (All scripture quotations are from the NIV Study Bible, Copyright 1985 by the Zondervan Corporation.)

The intention of this format is to encourage day by day reflections on a kingdom of God essential biblical truth, idea and theme in such a way that prompts deeper understanding and wisdom application. (The reflection passages each week will vary between 4 and 6 days.)

Merriam - Webster Definition of Essential:
Noun
Something necessary, indispensable, or unavoidable.

ABOVE ALL, BELIEVE

"For God so loved the world that He gave his one and only Son, that whoever **believes** in Him shall not perish but have eternal life." John 3:16

Perhaps John 3:16 is the most quoted verse in the New Testament. Jesus declares this while talking to Nicodemus, a member of the Jewish ruling council, answering his question - "How can this be?" (3:9) Nicodemus has approached Jesus under the cover of night saying, "Rabbi, we know you are a teacher who has come from God. For no one could perform the miraculous signs You are doing if God were not with Him." (John 3:1 - 2)

Read the entire conversation in John 3:1 - 21, and underline the following words: *truth, believe, believes, believed.* The repetition of these keywords indicate the connection between truth and belief. What does truth have to do with believing?

Look at John 3:21.

What does belief look like?

Prayer: Dear LORD, show me how to live by the truth so that Your truth may be seen plainly. Amen

Week 1, Day 2 Reflection

Essential 1: Believe

Try thinking about this statement: Belief must be seen in order to be belief.

You may tell me that you believe, but what is the evidence that activates true belief? That is why John the writer follows the Nicodemus conversation with John the Baptist's testimony. Read John 3:22 - 36 What is the proof that reveals that John is a believer of truth? (Hint: Reread John 3: 31-36 and notice the repetition of "above all.")

Belief without action is not true belief. John the Baptist had an opportunity to testify about himself and the sacrificial life he lived in the wilderness attracting hundreds of people to be baptized. However, when questioned he told the truth - "I am not the Christ but sent ahead of Him … He must become greater; I must become less." (John 3: 27, 30)

Are you a believer in Jesus Christ? What is your testimony?

Prayer: Thank Jesus for His grace and mercy and tell Him that you want to reflect His truth that is the light of the world.

Week 1, Day 3 Reflection

Essential 1: Believe

Are you intimidated by the first two days thinking about belief? Read Mark 9:14 - 24.

In this passage the disciples fail in the attempt to heal a boy with an evil spirit. What does Jesus say to them? Copy verse 19 below:

Ouch! What do you think were the assumptions the disciples had made that led to their failure?

Now reread Mark 9:21 - 24. The father simply asked Jesus to heal his son by saying, "if you can do anything, take pity on us and help us." Write Jesus' reply below:

How does the father respond? "I do ...

Prayer: Pray this simple prayer: Dear Jesus, "I do believe; help me overcome my unbelief."

Week 1, Day 4 Reflection

Essential 1: Believe

Read Mark 9:28 - 29
The disciples privately ask Jesus, "Why couldn't we drive out [the evil spirit?] What was Jesus' reply?

Now read Luke 9:28 - 41
Where was Jesus when the disciples could not drive out the evil spirit? (Luke 9:28)

What was Jesus doing on the mountain? (Luke 9:28)

Jesus modeled that belief begins with prayer. There are many times in the gospels that reveal Jesus' prayer life praying for His disciples and for God's will to be done.

We don't know the rest of the story of the father and son. However, we have the conversation between Jesus and His disciples about the power of prayer in Jesus' explanation in Mark 9:29. "This kind can come out only by prayer."

A group of men met weekly in my living room studying God's word and praying for each other. One morning as we finished our study and asked for prayer, one of the men requested for us to pray for him. He explained that he had recently been diagnosed with Multiple Sclerosis, and he had been told that the meds would prevent him from having children. So, we all gathered around him as he knelt, and we put our hands on him praying for him while he sobbed. We continued to pray for him week after week. Months later when we ended our weekly study and went to prayer, this man said he had some news - his wife was pregnant! We all burst out with amazement and happy tears. Now after 20+ years this same man who suffers from MS has three healthy children.

Mark 9:23 "Everything is possible for him who believes."

In John 1:12 John writes, "... all who received [Jesus], to those who believed in His name, He gave the right to become children of God..."

Believing in Jesus Christ's name is believing in the Messiah who is your Savior. Also believing in Jesus gives us access to God the Father as His children. And like all fathers, your Heavenly Father will care for you as His child.

Prayer: Tell your Heavenly Father that you believe in Jesus as your Savior, and ask Him to help you in your unbelief.

Week 1, Day 5 Reflection

Essential 1: Believe

Read John 2:11 and 22
Do you see the interesting contrast between these verses?
John 2:11 "... and His disciples put their faith in Him."
John 2:22 "...Then they believed the Scripture and the words that Jesus had spoken."

John 2:11 is in the context of Jesus' first miracle turning water into wine. John 2:22 is in the context of what happened after he was raised from the dead.

What would you say is the contrast between these two statements?

At the beginning of their 3 years of training and following Jesus, the disciples put their faith in their leader, but they still needed help with their unbelief. Does that describe you? You may have faith in Jesus and how he lived his life, but He has not changed you because you still are dedicated to your own plan for your life making you cautious, and rarely stepping out in faith.

Nicodemus walked away from his conversation with Jesus without acting on believing in Jesus. However, after Jesus dies on the cross, Nicodemus shows up with 75 pounds of myrrh and aloes to take Jesus' body and prepare it in accordance with Jewish burial customs. (John 19:39 - 42) Scripture does not say anything about Nicodemus after those verses. Yet, we can surmise that Nicodemus had to remember Jesus' words to him three years ago when he saw Jesus lifted up on the cross. So, Nicodemus took action to honor the body of Christ.

> *"Just as Moses lifted up the snake in the desert, so the Son of Man must be lifted up, that everyone who believes in Him may have eternal life. For God so loved the world that He gave His one and only Son, that whoever **believes in Him** shall not perish but have eternal life." (John 3:15 - 16)*

Belief is a way of life, not a one time commitment. As imperfect and sinful people we struggle with evil. However, because Jesus has died for our imperfections and sins we can cry out to Him and seek to live by that truth by believing in Jesus' name. Having watched Jesus die on the cross and then meeting Him as resurrected Savior, the disciples activated their belief in living by the truth and changing the world for the Gospel.

Prayer: Thank God for the full Word of God and the witness of those who have modeled living by the truth. Tell Him that you want to act on your faith and belief according to His will, not your will.

Week 1, Day 6 Reflection

Essential 1: Believe

"The One who comes from above is **above all**; the one who is from the earth belongs to the earth, and speaks as one from the earth. The One who comes from heaven is **above all.** He testifies to what He has seen and heard, but no one accepts His testimony. The man who has accepted it has certified that God is truthful. For the One whom God has sent speaks the words of God, for God gives the Spirit without limit...Whoever believes in the Son has eternal life, but whoever rejects the Son will not see life, for God's wrath remains in him." (John 3:31 – 34, 36)

This testimony of John the Baptist right after he declared that Jesus "must become greater; I must become less." (John 3:30) makes it clear that believing in the One who is **above all** is paramount. In other words, you may strive to perfect your skills of being faithful in performing each of the biblical essential traits in this devotional guide, but miss that believing in the Son is **above all else.** In fact, every one of the weekly devotional essentials flow out of this first and foremost truth.

Prayer: So, before you turn the page to Week 2, acknowledge that Jesus is the One who is **above all**, the Son of God who speaks the truth. And, like John the Baptist, you desire that Jesus become greater in your life.

"ABOVE ALL ELSE, GUARD YOUR HEART"

"Above all else, **guard your heart,** for it is the wellspring of your life." Proverbs 4:23

What is a wellspring? In general a wellspring is a source of continual and dependable supply of clean water. The word "Wellspring" connects two words that when put together connote a continuous flow of unpolluted clean water. The comparison of one's heart with a wellspring may be obscure for you because your clean water flows through bathrooms, kitchens and outdoor faucets. We don't fret about water pollution taking for granted the plumbing that connects to reservoirs and artesian wells fed by underground springs. However, without those springs we would not survive for very long.

Hezekiah, King of Judah, "trusted in the LORD, God of Israel." (2Kings 18:5) In the fourteenth year of his reign, the king of Assyria attacked all the fortified cities of Judah and captured them. Then the king of Assyria and his armies approached Jerusalem stopping at the aqueduct of the Upper Pool, the water source for Jerusalem. Instead of attacking the walls of the city, the armies turned off the supply of water and began a siege waging a propaganda war of words demanding that the people surrender. The siege lasted three years. Sensing that the people of Jerusalem were desperate, the king of Assyria sent a message to Hezekiah and the people of Jerusalem:

"Make peace with me and come out to me. Then every one of you will eat from his own vine and fig tree and **drink water from his own [well.]**" (2Kings 18:31) You can read the full remarkable story of what happened in 2Kings 18:1 - 19:37.

What does the image of a wellspring have to do with your heart? Throughout scripture "heart" represents one's essence, your core beliefs and passions. Perhaps the most quoted example of a scripture use of "heart" is David's cry out in Psalm 51:10: "Create in me a pure heart, O God and renew a steadfast spirit within me." (NIV) Throughout his compelling Psalm, David is confessing that his heart had been polluted by his sin of committing adultery and murder. He recognized that a polluted heart will poison and eventually kill him. So, how did he respond to that recognition? Read Psalm 51 and underline or highlight David's humble confession and sincere requests beginning with the following verbs: "Have mercy, Wash away, Cleanse me, Create in me, Restore me, Save me."

Have you allowed your wellspring to become polluted through your attitudes, thoughts, actions, and words? While we may not have literally committed adultery or murder, our attitudes, thoughts and words little by little pollute and poison your heart beliefs and passions. That is why Solomon, King David's son, instructs his son and by extension us to "above all else guard your heart." Solomon knows how easy it is to corrupt our inner heart.

I visited a missionary who lived in Kurungu, Kenya. Kurungu is in the middle of a vast desert in northwest Kenya. For most of each year the high mountains, huge sand hills and wide riverbeds remain dry and desolate. We actually were able to slide down sand hills into the riverbed below as if the sand was snow. However, my missionary friend told me about what happens each year in the short rainy season. The rain floods riverbeds overflowing into the desert creating a massive lake full of catfish. So, where did the catfish come from? The answer is that for most of each year the catfish burrow deep in the mud and hibernate. Then when the rains come they become a mass of writhing, muddy fish you can catch with your hands. However, If you were to catch one and try to filet, cook and eat it, your mouth would fill up with muddy sand, because the fish have been polluted by the mud they hibernated in.

What does the wellspring of your heart hold? Outwardly your life may appear to be a pristine landscape of purity. But what if someone could look into the depths of your heart? Would there be a mess of muddy sins or a well of clean water?

How should you guard your heart? Like David, go before God through prayer asking for mercy and forgiveness, asking God to create in you a pure heart. David writes in Psalm 51:17 "The sacrifices of God are a broken spirit; a broken and contrite heart..."

Then going forward in God's grace protect your heart above all else by asking God each morning to create in you a pure heart. And every night before going to bed ask the Holy Spirit to influence you to "desire truth in the inner parts; ...[and] teach you wisdom in the inmost place" (Psalm 51:6) because your " heart is the wellspring of [your] life." (Proverbs 4:23)

Prayer: Father God, have mercy according to your love. Wash away my impure attitudes, thoughts, words and actions. Create in me a clean heart as I confess my sinful nature. Forgive me and purify me from all unrighteousness.

Encouragement
God is for you, not against you. He has provided the Holy Spirit as your counselor who patiently points you to God's mercy and restoration that comes through confession.

Week 2, Day 2 Reflection
Essential 2: "Above all else, Guard Your Heart"

Read: 1John 1:5 - 10

- What is the problem? (v. 6, 8)

- What is the solution? (v. 7, 9)

Focus on 1John 1:9

'If we confess our sins, He is faithful and just and will forgive us our sins, and **purify** us from all unrighteousness."

God is faithful and just! How is he faithful? Justice is a legal term that communicates the assignment of punishment for breaking the law. How is God just? (Hint: Who received the punishment for your past, present and future sins?)

Examine your heart. What are the struggles you have with pollution of your thoughts and attitudes?

Write below a prayer confessing those thoughts and attitudes.

Week 2, Day 3 Reflection
Essential 2: "Above all else, Guard Your Heart" Proverbs 4:23

My mother often quoted Numbers 32:23b to her children. "...be sure your sins will find you out." Despite her warnings, I buried my sins and convinced myself that they were permanently gone. Then I worked hard at deleting the sins from my memory by believing my lies. But those lies increased the corruption of my heart. Then one day, I was confronted by someone whom I had sinned against, and suddenly all those buried lies and sins drove me to my knees, weeping over the memories of my lies and sins.

Have you buried your sin? Have you deceived people and lied about past sins? Like the Kurungru filthy catfish, those sins are hibernating in your muddy deceits waiting to come out.

King David had shrewdly buried his sin of adultery by arranging for Bathsheba's husband to be put on the front lines of battle ensuring that he would be killed. He thought that the sin would never find him out until the prophet Nathan came to him and exposed his horrendous sins of adultery and murder. Convicted, David petitioned the LORD to "Wash away all my iniquity and cleanse me from my sin." (Psalm 51: 2) He then wrote "For I know my transgressions, and my sin is always before me." (Psalm 51:3)

Unconfessed sin will always find you out, revealing inescapable and painful regrets.

While sin slowly pollutes and eats away at your heart, it imprisons you and compromises your health causing you to miss out on God's good intentions for your flourishing and wellbeing.

As a teenager working in New York City, I worked for a man I admired. One day I was instructed to take one of the company trucks full of new office furniture and deliver the furniture in lower Manhatten. I felt important and cocky about being trusted to drive a large truck in New York City. Near Wall Street, I made a right hand turn on a narrow street, and I heard an awful noise on the right side panel of the truck. Stopping, I went out to inspect the damage. I had hit a parked truck causing a huge concave dent. Climbing up in the truck, I tried to kick the dent out. I thought if I don't find a way to cover up this accident I would be demoted from doing deliveries.

So, on the way back to the garage I worked out a plan to lie about the accident. I drove the truck into the garage and parked it next to a pole on the right side. When the next driver found the damaged truck the next day, he came to me to ask about the damage. I lied, telling him that when I brought it to the garage, I allowed the attendant to park it, and he must have caused the damage.

That lie came back to haunt me 40 years later, when I had to speak in a Christian School Chapel about telling the truth. Suddenly, I remembered that lie and knew that I had to come clean. So, for the first time in 40 years I confessed the lie in my talk as their Principal, telling the students "be sure your sins will find you out."

What buried sins do you need to confess?

God is for you, not against you. He wants you to be free from past regrets so that you become free to experience what good he has for you.

Prayer: Forgiving Lord, I confess my past sins that I have hid in my heart. (Then name them.)
Ask God to create in you a pure heart.

Week 2, Day 4 Reflection

Essential 2: "Above all else, Guard Your Heart" Proverbs 4:23
Word Search "heart"

In the NIV Study Bible there are at least 725 verses that have the word "heart." Read each of the three verses listed below from Psalms, and choose one to pray over, asking God to help you apply and understand how to guard your heart.

Psalm 37:4
Psalm 53:1
Psalm 86:11

Week 2, Day 5 Reflection

Essential 2: "Above all else, Guard Your Heart" Proverbs 4:23
Word Search "heart"

Read each of the verses below from Proverbs, and choose one to pray over, asking God to help you apply and understand how to guard your heart.

Proverbs 14:30
Proverbs 16:23
Proverbs 27:19

Week 2, Day 6 Reflection

Essential 2: "Above all else, Guard Your Heart" Proverbs 4:23
Word Search "heart"

Read each of the verses below from the New Testament, and choose one to pray over, asking God to help you apply and understand how to guard your heart.

Matthew 6:21
Hebrews 4:12

ABOVE ALL ELSE, "PRAY CONTINUALLY"

1 Thessalonians 5:17

Personally, I struggle with prayer mostly because I am impatient. Too often I come to God in prayer with a list of requests and a timeline in mind for receiving an answer, as if I am ordering packages in my Amazon.com cart sometimes for same day delivery, other times overnight delivery, and sometimes as soon as possible delivery.

Describe below your prayer practice or routine.

If somehow you recorded and saved your prayers, what would you discover? Try this week to daily journal your prayers by writing them down. (See Addendum A)

Note: Each devotional this week will suggest a prompt for your prayer journal in Addendum A.

Tonight just before you go to bed write in your prayer journal thanking God for something that happened today.

Week 3, Day 2 Reflection

Essential 3: Above all else, "pray continually" 1Thessalonians 5:17

Read Matthew 6:9 - 13 below:

> Our Father in heaven,
> hallowed be your name,
> your kingdom come,
> your will be done
> on earth as it is in heaven.
> Give us today our daily bread.
> Forgive us our debts
> as we also have forgiven our debtors.
> And lead us not into temptation,
> But deliver us from the evil one.

How many sentences are there in this prayer? _____

How many requests are there in this prayer? _____

List the requests below.

"hallowed _____,

your _____,

your _____,

on _____."

Give _____.

Forgive _____, as

_____.

And _____,

but _____.

Who is the focus of the first sentence?

Who is the focus of the second sentence?

What is the condition cited in the third sentence? In other words, the request is conditional to what actions?

What is the compound request of the last sentence?

Prayer: In your prayer journal personalize your prayer following the order of the LORD"S Prayer. (Hint: Review the questions above.)

Week 3, Day 3 Reflection

Essential 3: Above all else, "pray continually" 1Thessalonians 5:17

Read Ephesians 3:14 - 21 below and answer the questions below the passage.

> "…I kneel before the Father, from whom his whole family in heaven and on earth derives its name. I pray that out of his glorious riches, he may strengthen you with power through his Spirit in your inner being so that Christ may dwell in your hearts through faith. And I pray that you, being rooted and established in love, may have power with all the saints, to grasp how wide and long and high and deep is the love of Christ, and to know this love that surpasses knowledge - that you may be filled to the measure of all the fullness of God.
>
> "Now to him who is able to do immeasurably more than all we ask, or imagine, according to his power that is at work within us, to him be the glory in the church and

in Christ Jesus throughout all generations, for ever and
ever! Amen"

What is Paul's posture in prayer?

Who is Paul addressing in this prayer? (Note that it is the same at the start
of the LORD'S Prayer.)

Who is Paul praying for?

What are the requests? Use your own words

"I pray that...

"And I pray that...

Who is the focus of the last sentence of Paul's prayer? Summarize the
closing idea in the prayer.

What are the similarities in this prayer to the LORD'S Prayer?

Prayer journal: Write a prayer (like the Ephesians 3:14 - 21 prayer) about
someone(s) you care about.

Week 3, Day 4 Reflection

Essential 3: Above all else, "pray continually" 1Thessalonians 5:17

The more I try to pray, the more I recognize that I tend to ask God to change the situations in my life instead of changing me. Too often I want to exchange God's plans for my plans. However, like a loving father God patiently waits for me to ask God to change me.

Use the Hillsong lyrics below from the song Hosanna to help you ask God to change you.

"Heal my heart, make it clean.

Open my eyes to the things unseen.

Show me how to love like you have loved me.

Break my heart for what breaks yours.

Everything I am for your Kingdom's cause,

As I walk earth to eternity."

Prayer journal: Write a prayer like the lyrics above asking God to change you. (Go ahead and use some of the same words but be more specific about what you want God to change in you.)

Week 3, Day 5 Reflection

Essential 3: Above all else, "pray continually" 1Thessalonians 5:17

Read Luke 18:1 - 8
How does this instruction from Jesus illustrate praying continually?

(Luke 18:1) Luke writes that Jesus told his disciples a parable to ...

(Luke 18:2-3) Who are the two characters of this parable?

(Luke 18:4-5) Why does the Judge give in?

(Luke 18:6-8) What is the moral/meaning of this parable?

God wants his children to pray continually for their requests for justice to be done because we are demonstrating our faith in God. Keep asking!

Prayer journal: In your journal write a prayer about someone you know who needs daily prayer because of their deep needs or circumstances.

Week 3, Day 6 Reflection

Essential 3: Above all else, "pray continually" 1Thessalonians 5:17
Review your prayer journal, and then using what you have learned about prayer create an outline you can use for your daily prayer time. Write the outline down so that you can review it each day before your time of prayer.

ABOVE ALL, "FOR ME TO LIVE IS..."

"For me, to live is Christ, and to die is gain." Philippians 1:21

How would you complete the statement "For me, to live is…? Be honest. When you awakened this morning, what were you looking forward to? What is the most important thing in your life right now? What dream or passion do you have that is above all else in your life?

How would you prioritize the following list starting with the most valuable down to least valuable?

Prayer, Listening, Worship, Humility, Friends, Popularity, Recognition, Grade Point Average, Health, Money, Success

Surveys have demonstrated that *Friends* would top the list for most teens. *Prayer, Listening* and *Worship* would be low on the list after *Health, Money, Popularity, Recognition, Success and Humility*, with *Grade Point Average* somewhere in the middle. In fact, there is nothing wrong with any of the values on the list, but what value should be above all others? That is the essence of Paul's striking statement, "For me, to live is Christ, and to die is gain." We flippantly use the phrase "to die" often as an emphasis. For example we may say "I am dying for a Big Mac because I am so hungry." That is not what Paul is doing when he writes, "I eagerly expect and hope that I will in no way be ashamed, but will have sufficient courage so that now as always Christ will be exalted in my body whether by life or by death." (Philippians 1:20)

Paul's view on what is ultimately valuable is the opposite of the world's view. The world thinks that the essence of life is having meaningful relationships that provide wealth and wellbeing. As citizens of the world we experience the pull for us to do almost anything to be popular, avoid loneliness and follow our dreams. We naturally seek recognition and self-fulfillment in our friendships. But Paul states that real life comes from our relationship with Christ. This eternal relationship first deals with our sins and then transforms our hearts to value others above ourselves.

When I was 28, I made physical fitness my highest value because I was woefully overweight. So, I decided to begin running daily. I mapped out a three miles course near my apartment. The first day I could only jog a mile because I was out of shape. However, in three months I could easily run 3 miles, and I decided to make two primary goals - run in a 10K race and enter a marathon. As I focused every day on my training, I felt stronger and stronger. Soon I was running six to eight miles a day. I knew I was taking control of my body and getting into the best shape of my life. The week before my 10K I tested my fitness by running 22 miles in one day, proving I was ready to achieve my yearlong goals.

The race day came, and I felt confident. At the start I charged out with the leaders. As I reached half way into the race, I began to feel the heat and humidity of the day. I remember becoming dizzy, but I continued to push myself. That was the last thing I remember. I am told that in the last mile I began to lose control of my form, staggering to the finish line. My brother who was at the finish line ran out to help me, but I was already unconscious. I don't remember the ambulance ride to the hospital. By the time I reached the hospital, my body temperature was 106 and I was in a coma.

I suffered heat stroke and kidney failure. When I came out of the coma, I found myself in the ICU incapable of controlling even the most basic body functions. There I was in the hospital for 6 weeks after believing I was invincible and in control of my body. I had decided that for me to live was to get into shape and maintain fitness, but instead I had almost killed myself. In that mindset I had resolved for me to live is to be in great fitness and to die was not an option until it almost became a consequence.

What are you prepared to die for? Your list of values will be eternally aligned naturally only when you put Christ first, not your desires or your passions.

Encouragement: Read Psalm 37:4 "Delight yourself in the LORD and He will give you the desires of your heart." This verse is not a promise. King David is declaring that when you commit to delighting in God's plan for you, the desires of your heart will align with God's good and perfect will for you.

Prayer: Dear Lord Jesus, help me to above all live for you and your eternal kingdom everyday. Show me your will for this day and everyday going forward. Amen.

Week 4, Day 2 Reflection

Essential 4: Above all, "For me to live is…" Philippians 1:21

Read and highlight Philippians 1:9 - 11. Then personalize Paul's prayer for yourself by changing the pronouns. See my example below:

> LORD, may my love abound more and more in knowledge and depth of insight, so that I may be able to discern what is best and may be pure and blameless until the day of Christ. Fill me with the fruit of righteousness that comes from You Lord Jesus - to the glory and praise of God the Father.

Perhaps this prayer should be a daily prayer that you memorize.

Week 4, Day 3 Reflection

Essential 4: Above all, "For me to live is..." Philippians 1:21

How you complete the sentence - "For me to live is..." - will put you on a **pathway** that becomes your **way** of life. On the other hand, you can try to map out your own **way** by setting your own goals like I did when I was 28 feeling more and more confident in my progress and my control of my life, all the while not realizing that I was headed for the absolute opposite outcome of those goals.

Many of Solomon's Proverbs use the metaphor of **ways, paths or pathways**. Read each of the Proverbs listed below and then restate the main idea.

> The LORD detests the **way** of the wicked, but He loves those who pursue righteousness. Stern discipline awaits him who leaves the **path**; he who hates correction will die. Proverbs 15: 9 - 10
> Main Idea:

> The **path** of life leads upward for the wise to keep him from going down to the grave. Proverbs 15:24
> Main Idea:

> Trust in the LORD with all your heart and lean not on your own understanding; in all your **ways** acknowledge Him, and He will make your **paths** straight. Proverbs 3:5 - 6
> Main Idea:

Prayer: Which main idea do you need to pray about asking God for understanding of the **way** you need to go today?

Week 4, Day 4 Reflection

Essential 4:Above all, "For me to live is…" Philippians 1:21

Read Philippians 1:18b - 23

Paul is writing this letter to the believers in Philippi thanking them for their generous gifts upon learning that Paul was in prison. Instead of complaining about his condition, Paul sees his circumstances as a **way** for advancing the Gospel. Exalting Christ was his **way** of life regardless of the suffering and persecution. Literally, Paul's life was threatened, yet he declared that to die would be gain not loss. Gain for what? Look at verses 22 - 23 and identify Paul's desire.

"I am torn between the two: I desire to _____ which is better by far."

Why is that better by far?

How does that statement emphasize and amplify his statement: "For me to live is Christ?"

Prayer: Life giving Jesus, show me the better way for me this day by reminding me that today is one more day toward eternal life. Amen

Week 4, Day 5 Reflection

Priority 4: Above all, "For me to live is…" Philippians 1:21

Read Philippians 2:5 - 11

What was the gain that Christ Jesus modeled and Paul imitated?

Read Philippians 4:4 - 8 and use this passage to inform your prayer

Prayer: LORD Jesus, I want to above all else seek "by prayer and petition, [and] thanksgiving... whatever is **true**, whatever is **noble**, whatever is **right**, whatever is **pure**, whatever is **lovely**, whatever is **admirable**, [and whatever] is **excellent or praiseworthy**." Guide me in the way of Jesus this day. Amen

From which "whatever is" list – true, noble, right, pure, lovely, admirable, excellent, praiseworthy - do you need to seek today?

ABOVE ALL, BE-ATTITUDES

"Blessed are the pure in heart, for they will see God." Matthew 5:8

Before reading on, answer these two questions:

What is an attitude?

From where does an attitude originate?

Jesus, In His Sermon on the Mount, highlighted nine beatitudes that highlight postures or attitudes that will ultimately lead to experiencing blessings. (See Matthew 5:3 - 11) Each of the beatitudes originates from a heart's desire to live out eternal priorities.

The Apostle Paul in his letter to the Ephesians uses the word "attitude" when he focuses on the importance of being "made new in the attitude of [our] minds." (Ephesians 4:23) He instructs that every believer needs to "put off" our old self and "put on the new self." This idea suggests that an attitude comes from our inner self-focused thoughts, and they can be made new by looking back at "your former way of life" by putting off the old self and putting on a new attitude. Do you remember being instructed by a parent or coach to "change your attitude?" That instruction recognizes that you have the ability to put off a negative attitude and replace it with a positive attitude. According to Paul we should "get rid of (put off) all bitterness, rage and anger, brawling and slander, along with every form of malice, and put on [kindness and compassion] toward one another, forgiving each other, just as in Christ God forgave you…[being] imitators of God…and liv[ing] a life of love." (Ephesians 4:31 – 5:2)

Looking back at my teenage years, I still feel embarrassed about my selfish attitudes. For example, as a high school sophomore I mainly warmed the bench of my high school football team. However, I did play on the kickoff team each game. My goal was to earn a varsity letter so that I could buy and wear a varsity letter jacket. That meant I had to minimally participate in one play for half of the season's game quarters. So my focus was on making sure the stats person knew that I had played on the kickoff team. I remember with great embarrassment during halftime when the head coach was speaking passionately to the team. Instead of listening I was in the back making sure that the stats person had recorded my first half playing time. Suddenly, the head coach stopped talking and called me out about my selfish attitude. Everyone on the team turned to see my embarrassing selfish pursuit of my heart's desire for earning a letter jacket.

There is much in our lives that we have no choice about. We can't change our skin color, or our DNA, our fingerprints, where we were born, our birth date, and our number of days. However, we can choose and change our attitudes. An attitude is a choice that either curses or blesses. Because it is a choice, we have the opportunity to choose an "Above All Be-Attitude." That is to say, above all the negative desires that produce bad attitudes I can choose good 'Be-Attitudes' that have power to bless not curse. Choosing positive 'Be-Attitudes' like ones listed below will influence and enhance your self-control and maturity.

> Be Humble
> Be Grateful
> Be Positive
> Be Clean

Be Merciful
Be A Peacemaker
Be Prayerful
Be Faithful

Prayer: Father God, as you cleanse my heart and mind, help me to put off my old self and choose to be made new, choosing Be-Attitudes that bless others, and choosing above all to "live a life of love, just as Christ loved [me]." (Ephesians 5:2)

Encouragement: Everyday you have the power to choose positive attitudes allowing you to be free of negative thoughts.

Week 5, Day 2 Reflection

Essential 5: Above All Be-Attitudes

From the list of positive attitudes of Day 1 which 'Be-Attitude' do you need to choose today?

Be Humble
Be Grateful
Be Positive
Be Clean
Be Merciful
Be A Peacemaker
Be Prayerful
Be Faithful

Prayer: Holy Spirit, remind me of my choice to put on a positive Be-Attitude throughout today.

How did the day go?

Week 5, Day 3 Reflection

Essential 5: Above All Be-Attitudes

Read Ephesians 4:22, 25, 31 and 5:3 - 4. Then list what needs to be put off or get rid of in the verses below.

Verse 4:22: Put off

Verse 4:25: Put off

Verse 4:31: Get rid of

Verses 5:3 - 4: Get rid of

Which one of these negative attitudes do you need to get rid of first?

Prayer: Lord help me to permanently put off and get rid of

_____.

Week 5, Day 4 Reflection

Essential 5: Above All Be-Attitudes

Read Ephesians 4:24, 32, and 5:2, 8 - 10 and list what needs to be permanently put on in place of the negative attitudes.

Verses 4:24

Verse 4:32

Verses 5:2, 8-10

Prayer: As I choose an attitude to put on this day, teach me, Lord, how to live a life of love just like you have loved me. Amen

Week 5, Day 5 Reflection

Essential 5: Above All Be-Attitudes

Ephesians 5:8b and 11 - "Live as children of the light for the fruit of the light consists in all goodness...Have nothing to do with the fruitless deeds of darkness..."

Write below your answer to this question: How does "the fruit of the light" and "the fruitless deeds of darkness" describe the difference between positive attitudes and negative attitudes?

Prayer: Lord God, I want my attitudes to produce the fruit of goodness, righteousness, and truth today and every day. Help me to know what pleases you.

"ABOVE ALL, DO NOT SWEAR"

"Above all, my brothers and sisters **do not swear**—not by heaven or by earth or by anything else. All you need to say is a simple "Yes" or "No." Otherwise you will be condemned." James 5:12

Does James 5:12 confuse you?

James in Chapter 5 verses 7 - 12 writes about being patient in suffering, ending with his warning about not swearing in the last verse about the topic of personal suffering. These words about swearing are "above all" what he has written in the previous verses on suffering. Suffering has the ability to test our values. Suffering can influence our perspective, making us impatient, bitter and demanding. So James points to the Old Testament prophets who spoke in the name of the Lord and persevered despite being persecuted. They remained true in speaking God's words to the people. Then James cites Job's seemingly unfair intense catastrophe of losing everything including his children stating that in the midst of it all Job does not curse God. In fact, James declares that Job's suffering brought out an understanding that "the Lord is full of compassion and mercy."

Do you swear? When? Why?

Write your answers below. Don't read on until you have honestly answered these three questions.

1. Do you swear?

2. If you do, when do you usually swear?

3. Why do you swear? (There can be multiple reasons. Include all your reasons.)

Because language and words matter, James starts verse 12 with "Above all." Words communicate meanings, mindsets, emotions and motives. Why is it important to only "Let your 'Yes' be yes and your 'No,' no?" Swearing comes from your desire to curse a circumstance, or impress others, or flippantly use God's name to guarantee the truth of what you have spoken. If you are known as someone who can be truthful and humble, you will not need swear words when life seems unfair or disappointing, because you know that "the Lord is full of compassion and mercy." God is in control even when life seems out of control.

Reflect:
Review your answers to the three questions above. Then confess by asking God to help you clean up your language.

Encouragement: Deciding to be known as a person of your word will free you from the trap of always striving to impress others.

Week 6, Day 2 Reflection

Essential 6: "Above all...do not swear" James 5:12

"You shall not **misuse** the name of the LORD your God, for the LORD will not hold anyone guiltless who **misuses** His name." Exodus 20:7

Because Exodus 20:7 is the third commandment of the Ten Commandments given to Moses and the Israelites, it carries a lot of weight. Misusing the name of the LORD is breaking a holy commandment by swearing God's name falsely for one's personal gain. Leviticus 19:12 says, "Do not **swear falsely** by my name and so **profane** the name of your God. I am the LORD."

What does profane mean? Profane is a verb meaning to treat (something sacred) with abuse, irreverence, contempt, or for vulgar use. Because our culture profanes God's name in all kinds of ways, do you find yourself influenced to misuse God's name?

I play golf with a group of men some of which use profanity often. One man in particular is the king of colorful language including loudly profaning the name of Jesus Christ after missing a putt or miss hitting his approach shot. After having played in his foursome several times, I decided to approach him about my discomfort. When we were the only ones on the practice putting green, I asked if we could talk. Immediately, he said, "I know I use too many cuss words." I replied, "I can endure the colorful language, but I want to ask you to stop using 'Jesus Christ' as a curse because He is my Savior." He immediately apologized. From that point on he no longer used swear words and the name of Jesus when we played together. Rather than him trying to avoid playing with me, we actually became good friends, enjoying playing together often. He has even agreed to be fined if he misuses the name of Jesus, joking that he hates losing money more than he likes swearing.

Now think about the second part of the third commandment that states "the LORD will **not hold** any one guiltless who misuses His name." Misusing God's name leads to a charge of guilty against you. Have you slipped into profanity by abusing God's name? Guilt can be healthy when it makes you uncomfortable causing you to confess and ask to be restored. The good news of the Gospel is that the law that condemns you now offers God's forgiveness and redemption.

Prayer: Almighty God, forgive me for misusing your name for my gain. I want everything I say to be true and respectful. Thank you for your saving grace and mercy. Amen

Week 6, Day 3 Reflection

Essential 6: "Above all...do not swear" James 5:12

For the most part, I have made it a practice to not swear, but I remember a lesson about my mindless swearing in order to get approval from others. When I became a high school teacher and football coach after college influenced by other coaches older than me, I wanted to be accepted. Each day before and after practice while in our coaches' locker room we would talk about our athletes and the quality of each practice. Most of the coaches used colorful language regularly. Even though it was 50 years ago, I vividly remember when I voiced an opinion using the same colorful language. Immediately, the locker room went from boisterous conversation to dead quiet. With everyone looking at me, the head coach said, "Don't use that word! That word does not fit with who you are."

How does your language demonstrate who you are?

British author and pastor Sam Allberry comments on the swearing of oaths and misusing the name of the LORD in his book JAMES FOR YOU.

> The point is not that all oaths are always wrong, but that in everyday contexts oaths should be unnecessary. We shouldn't need to emphasize the truthfulness of a particular part of our speech, because *all our speech should be true and trustworthy...* Everything we say should be true. Our word should be enough. (JAMES FOR YOU, The Good Book Company, 2015, page 145, my emphasis)

Do your words demonstrate a desire to be true and trustworthy or are you using words to gain an advantage, to impress or deceive others?

Prayer: Holy Spirit, reveal to me how I use words in deceitful negative ways. Create in me a pure heart that rejects swearing. I want my language to demonstrate my commitment to being true and trustworthy. Amen

Week 6, Day 4 Reflection
Essential 6: "Above all… do not swear" James 5:12

"Do not let any unwholesome talk come out of your mouths, but only what is helpful for building others up…" Ephesians 4:29a

Another way to look at swearing is to label it unwholesome. Being wholesome is to be pure and uncorrupt, so being unwholesome is the opposite - to be corrupt and impure. Paul defines wholesome talk as being helpful for building others up. How are your words that come out of your mouth unwholesome by putting others down? Do you often put others down by insulting them or pointing out everything that is negative? What is your motive when you put others down?

Middle school and high school environments are often full of unwholesome talk. When I was in seventh grade, I was bullied by a group of boys. They made fun of my name. Whenever a teacher turned his back, they would take my homework, pencils, and pens and spill them on the floor. They made up a derogatory nickname and got the rest of the seventh grade to chant the name in the hallways and even in the classroom. One day, while our class was in the auditorium for a documentary movie, the boys got the entire class to begin to chant that nickname. So, I got up from my seat. Walked down the row to where the ringleader was sitting. I asked him to stop the chanting. When he smiled and repeated the nickname, I punched him in the face and walked back to my seat. Pandemonium broke out. The lights came on and a teacher escorted the two of us to the Principal's office. We both were sentenced to after school detention; however, from that moment on the bullying stopped.

My action definitely was not Christ-like; however, I share this story to give a clear picture of the power of unwholesome talk. That is why it is easy to be on the side of unwholesome words. Somehow, it is cool to make fun of others by putting them down saying, "I was only joking." To be sure this scenario doesn't just happen in middle school! Unwholesome talk is ubiquitous in all kinds of social contexts.

At the end of Ephesians 4, Paul writes: "Be kind and compassionate to one another, forgiving each other, just as in Christ God forgave you." (v.32) Because our God is kind, loving and compassionate, we are to imitate Him in all our language.

Prayer: Dear LORD, show me where I am guilty of being jealous, unkind, critical and negative towards others. Holy Spirit, help me to replace my unwholesome thoughts and words by being compassionate, forgiving others just as Christ has done for me. Amen

ABOVE ALL, "TRUST THE LORD WITH ALL..."

Above all, "Trust in the LORD with **all** your heart
and lean not on your own understanding;
⁶ in **all** your ways submit to him,
and he will make your paths straight

⁷ Do not be wise in your own eyes;
fear the LORD and shun evil.
⁸ This will bring health to your body
and nourishment to your bones." Proverbs 3:5 - 8

Did you know that the small word "all" is in 4,274 verses of the Bible? It appears 48 times in Proverbs alone. Such a little word denotes uncompromising synonyms like *entire, undivided,* or *whole.* How much should I trust in the Lord? Entirely! With no exceptions! Undividedly and wholly! How many of my different plans (ways) am I to submit to the Lord? All!

But Solomon is not implying that this instruction is a command. As a father, he is sharing this wisdom with his son, wanting him to have "many years...[of] peace and prosperity."

> "My son, do not forget my teaching, but keep my commands in your heart, for they will prolong your life many years and bring you peace and prosperity." Proverbs 3:1 - 2

So, Solomon points his son to pathways that will bring health and nourishment while at the same time warning him to **not** trust his own understanding only and to **not** be wise in his own eyes. Under those conditions, it is up to his son to apply his advice by trusting in the Lord with **all** his heart and keeping **all** his ways submitted to the Lord.

Our culture promises the exact opposite of Solomon's wisdom. We hear over and over at graduations, in TV shows, movies and advice columns that we are to above all trust our heart and our feelings. However, the wisest man ever, Solomon, warns that the pathway of worldly pursuit of autonomy actually leads to disorder, selfishness and disillusionment, not peace and prosperity.

God's word is full of stories in which people follow their heart and feelings. Two men that come to mind are Samson and David. Both men were called by God to trust in the Lord with all their heart. Despite God's clear calling and will, both of these men became wise in their own eyes and the result was disaster, brokenness and death.

Take a moment or two to ask yourself where you have been "wise in your eyes." When or where did you rebel against God's will thinking you knew better or thinking that you deserved what you wanted? When or where did you insist that you knew better than your parents? When or where have you insisted that your plans were better than the instructions from an authority over you? When have you insisted that your understanding is smarter than anyone else?

Good news! Your Father God patiently waits for you to come to your senses and trust in Him with **all** your heart and in **all** your ways submit to Him so that you can experience His blessings of health and prosperity. Ask the Holy Spirit to show you where you need to trust God with all your heart and all your ways.

Week 7, Day 2 Reflection

Essential 7: Above **all**

Read Samson's story in Judges Chapter 13:24 thru Chapter 16:31.

Questions:

What was Samson's assigned purpose?

How did he compromise his **above all** purpose?

Speculate why Samson compromised his calling. What was he thinking? How was he "being wise in his own eyes?"

Is there anything in this story that you can apply to your story? Why or why not?

Where or when have you compromised God's will for you by becoming wise in your own eyes?

Prayer: Use the answers to the questions above to thank God for His grace, and confess that you have leaned on your own understanding instead of trusting the LORD with all your heart.

Week 7, Day 3 Reflection

Essential 7: Above **all**

Read about David and Bathsheba's story in 2Samuel Chapter 11 thru Chapter 12:18.

Questions:

What was King David's assigned purpose?

How did he compromise his **above all** purpose?

Speculate why David compromised his calling. What was he thinking? How was he "being wise in his own eyes?"

Is there anything in this story that you can apply to your story? Why or why not?

Prayer: Use the answers to the questions above to thank God for His grace, and confess that you have leaned on your own understanding instead of trusting the LORD with all your heart.

Week 7, Day 4 Reflection

Essential 7: Above **all**

In chapter 15 of Luke's Gospel, Jesus tells the Parable of the Lost Son. The main character of the story is a son who demands his share of his father's estate and then leaves home, but following his heart desires results in squandering all of his wealth. I love how Jesus tells what happens next after the son finds himself filling his stomach with pods that the pigs were eating.

Then Jesus says, "When he came to *his senses*, he said… I am starving to death! I will set out and go back to my father and say to him: Father, I have sinned, against heaven and against you…" The consequence of following his own desires led him to come "to his senses." The result: Soberly, he confesses his sin of going astray by turning to his own way. (See Isaiah 53:6)

The Parable of the Lost Son is an illustration about being wise in your own eyes. Read the parable in Luke 15:11 - 32.

Questions:

How was the son an example of "being wise in [his] own eyes?"

Why did the son return home?

How did his father react to his return? Who does the father represent in this parable?

What is the moral of this parable?

Is there anything in this story that you can apply to your story? Why or why not?

Where/When have you compromised your faith by making demands and not trusting in the Lord with **all** your heart?

Prayer: Dear Father God, thank you for your loving grace despite my willful demands to go my own way. You, like the father in the Prodigal Son parable, patiently waited for me to come to my senses. Amen

ABOVE ALL, "BE RICH TOWARD GOD"

Luke 12:21b

"Do not store up for yourselves treasures on earth…But store up for yourselves treasures in heaven…For where your treasure is, there your heart will be, also." Matthew 6:19 - 21

What does being rich toward God look like? (Note: If I had asked you what does it mean to be rich, you likely would have no trouble answering. So, why is this question difficult to answer?)

In Luke's Gospel, 12:16 - 21, Jesus tells the Parable of the Rich Fool. The rich man produces a good crop and thinks to himself, "This is what I'll do. I will tear down my barns and build bigger ones, and there I will store all my grain and my goods. And I'll say to myself, 'You have plenty of good things laid up for many years. [So I will] take life easy; eat, drink, and be merry.' "But God said to him, 'You fool! This very night your life will be demanded from you.Then who will get what you have prepared for yourself?"

This parable, like most of the parables told by Jesus, challenges our worldview. Do you want to ask, "What is wrong with planning for the future and storing up wealth?" And you mean for that question to be rhetorical because you think you know the answer. However ask yourself, who is the rich man talking to when he says, "This is what I'll do... I'll store all my grain...and take life easy; eat, drink and be merry?" What makes this plan foolish? Who is the treasure for? Why is that foolish?

Well, little did the rich fool know that that very night his "life will be demanded" for all eternity. Then Jesus states the lesson intended in the parable, "This is how it will be with anyone who stores up things for himself [only] but is not **rich toward God**." (12:21b)

Matthew also highlights in (Matthew 6:19 – 21) Jesus' same teaching that we are "to store up...[our] treasures in heaven. [Because] where our treasure is, there our heart will be, also."

Before we can understand what it means to store up treasures in heaven, it is helpful to define "treasure." One definition for "treasure" is something of great worth or value. Using that definition, what are your treasures? List below the things of great worth or value that you treasure for yourself above all else.

Is it wrong to treasure things of great worth and value? Why or why not?

Prayer: Dear LORD, help me to discern between what is a temporary treasure and an eternal treasure so that I can begin to understand what it means to invest in being rich toward you. Amen

Week 8, Day 2 Reflection

Essential 8: Above all, "be rich toward God" Luke 12:21b

Being rich toward God starts with the following mindset. "So do not worry, saying. 'What shall we eat?' or 'What shall we drink?' or 'What shall we wear?' For the pagans run after all these things, and your heavenly Father knows that you need them. But seek first his kingdom and his righteousness, and all these things will be given to you as well."(Matthew 6:31 - 33) Verse 33 is a well known verse that emphasizes that we don't need to be anxious or worrisome because God knows our needs, freeing us to **seek first** God's eternal kingdom and righteousness. Why does God's kingdom and righteousness need to be first?

What do you worry about?

Explain the following simile: "Worry is like a rocking chair. It goes back and forth but goes nowhere."

What does being rich toward God have to do with seeking first God's kingdom and righteousness?

Write a sentence below that answers the following question: Today, what do you need to do to be rich toward God?

Prayer: Ask God to reveal to you how to increase your understanding of what it means to be rich toward God.

Week 8, Day 3 Reflection

Essential 8: Above all, "be rich toward God" Luke 12:21b

Read Mark 10:17 - 22 The Story of the Rich Young Man

> Note: In verse 17 a man "ran up" to Jesus and" fell on his knees." What does that description tell you about the young man?

> What was the question he blurted out to Jesus?

> How did Jesus answer him?

> What was the man's answer? Note: The man uses the tiny but huge word **"all."**

> How did Jesus reply to his proud full statement, **"all** these I have kept since I was a boy" statement?

> Why did the man's face fall?

> Why did the man go away?

Prayer: Dear Jesus, reveal to me where I am performing piously and proudly my obedient ways for myself only. Forgive me from convincing myself that my actions and wealth are all I need to be rich toward God. Amen

Week 8, Day 4 Reflection

Essential 8: Above all, "be rich toward God" Luke 12:21b

Read Luke 18:24 - 30

(Verse 24) What does Jesus say?

(Verse 26) What was the reaction of those who heard this?

(Verse 27 - 30) Jesus answers the question asked by disciples and others who heard Jesus speak by saying "What is impossible with men is possible with God." Jesus then affirms Peter's statement by agreeing that their sacrifices will receive abundant rewards "in this age" (worldly rewards) and "the age to come, (eternal life)." What is impossible with men but possible with God in Jesus' response to Peter? Reread verses 29 - 30 and then complete the statements below.

It was possible for the disciples to...

It was impossible for the disciples to ...

Prayer: Dear Jesus, thank you for your sacrifice of giving up heaven, your home and family to live a perfect life, submitting to the cross, and paying the price for my sins so that I have forgiveness and eternal life. Amen

Week 8, Day 5 Reflection

Essential 8: Above all, "be rich toward God" Luke 12:21b

Read Mark 12:41 - 44
How is the poor widow different from the rich young man?

Is the poor widow demonstrating what it means to be rich in God? Why or why not?

Prayer: Dear LORD, I acknowledge that often I put more faith in my savings account, and I often review my savings so that I feel secure. Teach me to be rich toward You reflecting on my security based on Your grace, forgiveness, and your promise of eternal life. Amen

ABOVE ALL ELSE, "LIVE BY THE SPIRIT"

"So I say, **live by the Spirit** and you will not gratify the desires of the sinful nature. Galatians 5:16

My golden retriever, Cooper, after much training, wants to be obedient, except when his nose takes over. When he is off leash, he has been trained to come back to me when I whistle, and he does except when his nose takes over. Every Sunday I take Cooper on a long walk behind the local middle school and elementary school. He knows that he will be off leash when we get to the middle school grounds, where he can run ahead exploring, all the while keeping me in view. If he gets too far away, I will whistle and he will come back to me, except when his nose takes over. One Sunday Cooper took off following his nose. Immediately I whistled, but he continued to run away. Sprinting from the back of the school, Cooper ran up to a busy road. Without hesitating he ran across the road causing cars to brake and swerve from hitting him. When he reached the other side of the road, he disappeared into a ditch. I crossed the road and ran to where I saw Cooper disappear. There he was rolling his body on top of a dead deer carcass. He had smelled the rotting carcass well over 200 yards away. I grabbed his collar pulling him off the putrid dead deer and leashed him. His fur was matted with deer flesh that almost caused me to wretch as I walked him home, where I had to bathe him twice to get rid of the smell.

Like Cooper I want to obey biblical instructions designed to keep me from gratifying my natural desires, but there are times when I ignore the Spirit and let my sinful nature take over. Cooper's sinful nature desires what is contrary to his training. Likewise, as a Christian, I follow my sinful nature causing me to do what I know is in conflict with the Spirit, and like Cooper I wallow in what stinks to high heaven.

What are the acts of a sinful nature? Paul gives us a list in Galatians 5:19 - 21: "sexual immorality, impurity and debauchery, idolatry and witchcraft, hatred, discord, jealousy, fits of rage, selfish ambition, dissensions, factions and envy, drunkenness, [and] orgies." Put a check mark next to the defined acts that you wrestle with.

Sexual immorality - Desiring to wallow in lust

Impurity - Unclean thoughts and actions

Debauchery - Extreme indulgence in sexual pleasures, drugs, and alcohol

Idolatry - Worship of anything other that God

Witchcraft - Communication with the devil or pagan rituals

Hatred - Extreme dislike

Discord - Active quarreling resulting in factions

Jealousy - Anger toward a rival or someone who you think has what you want

Fits of Anger - Easily angered

Selfish ambition - Chasing after what your own ego wants at the expense of others

Dissensions - Causing conflict between you and others for your gain

Factions - Creating a group against other groups

Envy - Wanting what someone else owns or has

Drunkenness - Frequent intoxication

Orgies - Drunken partying and excessive sexual participation

Prayer: Dear Father God, You know that I struggle with my sinful nature. I confess that I cannot control my desire to gratify the evil desires that are in conflict with my desire to live by the Spirit. Holy Spirit, convict me and point me to live by your Spirit. Amen

Week 9, Day 2 Reflection

Essential 9: Above all "live by the Spirit..." Galatians 5:16

As a Christian, the Holy Spirit dwells in you, teaching you how to not gratify your sinful nature. However, "we **all,** like sheep, have gone astray, each of us has turned to his own way; and the LORD has laid on Him [Jesus] the iniquity of us all." (Isaiah 53:6) Let me translate for the purpose of reflection. We all, like Cooper, have run away to wallow in our sinful nature, but our perfect Savior, Jesus Christ, has taken on our sins, exchanging his life for our salvation even though we stink to high heaven.

Does that mean we have a "free get out of jail" card every time we decide to gratify our sinful nature? No!

Cooper endured strong words of rebuke, two baths and more training. Like Cooper, we too are rebuked by God's word, the Spirit's conviction, and more training as we submit to the Lordship of Jesus. This process is called Sanctification, meaning that our submission to live by the Spirit is a process of growing into freedom from sin. This process will last until we meet Jesus.

Prayer: Thank you Lord Jesus for paying the penalty for the acts of my sinful nature. I choose to live by the Spirit's leading and counseling. Help me to grow to be sensitive to the Spirit's prompting day by day. Amen

Week 9, Day 3 Reflection

Essential 9: Above all "live by the Spirit..." Galatians 5:16

The Word of God is crammed full with stories of flawed followers of God. Each one had to learn the hard way about how sin corrupts all nature and the human heart. All of mankind are like sheep or Cooper turning away from God's way of life.

Imagine what it was like for the 12 disciples of Jesus following Him everyday for three years. Often Jesus rebuked them, challenging them as they followed their perfect Messiah. Perhaps, Peter is the best example of a proud but flawed disciple.

Read Luke 22:24 - 34

At the Last Supper as Jesus serves the disciples, they begin to question who will betray Jesus. Luke reports that that question led the disciples to begin to dispute among themselves "as to which of them was considered to be the greatest." Jesus rebukes the disciples, and that is when Peter proudly declares that he is ready to go with Jesus to jail and even death. (v.33) "Jesus answered, 'I tell you, Peter, before the rooster crows today, you will deny three times that you know me.'" (v.34) We know what happened because Peter's embarrassing denial of Jesus three times is reported in all four of the gospels.

Can you imagine how humiliated Peter must have felt? Peter the rock failed his LORD spectacularly! It is one thing to fail privately, but to have that failure recorded for all to read is devastating.

Encouragement: Your failure to consistently live by the Spirit pales next to Peter's failure. Yet we know that Peter is forgiven and restored by his risen Savior. No sin of yours is unforgivable! God has a plan for you as He restores you and sanctifies you.

Prayer: Write a prayer of confession that ends with asking God to continue His sanctifying work in you as you "live by the Spirit."

Week 9, Day 4 Reflection

Essential 9: Above all "live by the Spirit..." Galatians 5:16

Read John 21:15 - 19

Why does Jesus ask Peter three times if he truly loves Him?

What are the instructions that Jesus gives Peter each time Peter answers. (See verses 15b, 16b, 17b)

Verse 15b:

Verse 16b:

Verse 17b:

How do these instructions restore Peter?

God has a mission for each of us when we seek his forgiveness and restoration. That mission will be your way to "live by the Spirit."
Prayer: LORD Jesus, I love you with all my heart and I want to serve you by living by the Spirit. Show me how I am to be on mission for Your eternal kingdom. Amen

ABOVE ALL ELSE, "KEEP IN STEP WITH THE SPIRIT"

"Since we live by the Spirit, let us **keep in step with the Spirit**." Galatians 5:25

My wife would tell you that I am an impatient person, wound too tight, always pushing the pace when we go for a walk. Slow bumper to bumper traffic or long waits sitting in a doctor's office drives me out of my mind.

When I lived in Kenya teaching at Rift Valley Academy, I was chosen to help chaperon a group of 20 high school students to climb Mount Kilimanjaro. Mount Kilimanjaro is the largest freestanding mountain in the world with an elevation of 19,341 feet above sea level, and the footprint of the volcano is over 50 miles in circumference. Huge! Until then my experience with climbing mountains meant spending a day climbing to the summit, taking a few pictures, and hiking back down.

So, when our guides told us that our climb would take 4 days, I was skeptical. I thought, why can't we climb up in the morning and come down before night? The first day of our climb we climbed an easy ascent through lush rainforest arriving at cabins just below the tree line where we stayed overnight. The second day we climbed out of the rainforest beyond the tree line, and we had our first view of the summit. That night we stayed in A-frame huts at 14,000 feet. Before going to bed, our guides warned us that the next day would test our patience because of thin air and the risk of elevation sickness. We were told to prepare to climb pole, pole, (pol lee, pol lee) which is Swahili for slowly, slowly. The next day we began our trek walking painfully slow for me. I wanted to walk ahead because I wasn't feeling any different at the elevation, but because I was a leader I chose to put myself last of the group. It took all day to cross over the tundra up towards the peak. Finally, we reached the hostel that sits about 500 feet below the summit. The temperature was below freezing as we consumed a hot dinner prepared by our guides. At 1 a.m. the guides woke us to prepare to reach the top of Kilimanjaro. In the pitch dark night we could only manage taking two steps at a time with frequent rests. Once again I chose to be at the end. Needless to say, taking two steps and resting over and over again was painful for me. So, I began to sing out pole pole, pole pole to take my mind off how impatient I felt. All of the students joined me singing like we were on a march. After 4 hours of climbing just 500 feet, we arrived at the summit exactly at sunrise. What a spectacular view!

"Pole, pole" has become a reminder of my impatience. When I feel anxiety and frustration about the process of keeping "in step with the Spirit," I try to remember my pole, pole climb up Kilimanjaro. But instead of having guides setting the pace, I have the Spirit to keep in step with.

Reflect: Living by the Spirit implies keeping in step with the Spirit. Do you get impatient with the pace of your spiritual growth? Do you want to run ahead and get to the peak of your life?

Prayer: Thank you Lord for the Holy Spirit's patient guidance and work in my life. Remind me to be patient in keeping in step with the Spirit cultivating the fruit of love, joy, peace, *patience*, kindness, goodness, faithfulness, gentleness and self-control.

Week 10, Day 2 Reflection

Essential 10: Above all else "keep in step with the Spirit." Galatians 5:25

When I read Galatians 5:22 - 25 about the fruit of the Spirit, I want all the benefits of living by the Spirit immediately. "But the fruit of the Spirit is love, joy, peace, *patience*, kindness, goodness, faithfulness, gentleness and self-control." (Galatians 5:22) By calling these traits "fruit," Paul implies that the benefits of keeping in step with the Spirit imply a growth and ripening process over time. My impatient temperament has made learning to keep in step with the Spirit excruciating.

Which fruit of the Spirit on the list in Galatians 5:22 do you need to patiently cultivate, by asking the Spirit to remind you of the process? I put the fruit of *patience* in italics because that would be my answer. What is the fruit you need to work on cultivating?

Prayer: Holy Spirit, help me to cultivate _____ as I keep in step with your process. When I fail to keep in step, show me where I need to slow down or speed up to daily keep in the step with you. Amen

Week 10, Day 3 Reflection

Essential 10: Above all else "keep in step with the Spirit." Galatians 5:25

Jesus' disciples struggled with keeping in step with Jesus. Read Mark 9:14 - 32.

In Jesus' absence the disciples become entangled in an argument with teachers of the law. When Jesus arrived he asked about what the argument was about. What provoked the argument?

Why do you think this situation escalated into an argument?

How did Jesus react to the answer from the father who had asked the disciples to drive out an evil spirit in his son? (Mark 9: 17-19)

Why was Jesus upset with his disciples? (Mark 9:19) What is the key word in Jesus' reply?

Why do you think the disciples failed in trying to help the father and son?

Pause and think back to a time when you acted impulsively and selfishly to solve a problem or argument, and instead you caused a bigger problem or argument.

Prayer: Dear LORD, I confess that I choose to act impulsively and selfishly by being wise in my own eyes instead of seeking your wisdom. Amen

Week 10, Day 4 Reflection

Essential 10: Above all else "keep in step with the Spirit." Galatians 5:25

Reread Mark 9:21 - 32

How did Jesus handle the father and son?

How did Jesus react to the father saying, "I do believe; help me overcome my unbelief! (Mark 9:24b - 25)

When the disciples asked Jesus, "Why couldn't we drive it out?" (Mark 9:29) What was Jesus' answer?

Which of the fruits of the Spirit - love, joy, peace, patience, kindness, goodness, faithfulness, gentleness and self-control - would you say needed to be cultivated by the disciples in this situation?

Jesus modeled which of the fruits of the Spirit in the healing of the boy? Explain.

Prayer: Holy Spirit, I confess that I often run ahead of your work in me by willfully, not prayerfully, trying my best to be pious. Teach me to be prayerful, and patient as you help me in my unbelief. Amen

Week 10, Day 5 Reflection

Essential 10: Above all else "keep in step with the Spirit." Galatians 5:25

In Galatians 5:16 - 25 Paul points to two **ways** we can live: by the desires of our sinful nature or by the Spirit. One **way** leads to forfeiting an inheritance, and the other **way** leads to freedom from condemnation.

I purposefully put **way** in bold because it is a metaphor for how we choose to live. What does your **way** of life look like? Your **way** of life is a pathway you choose to walk on. Do you choose the **way** of gratifying the desires of your sinful nature or the **way** of keeping in step with the Spirit.

The **way** of your sinful nature will lead you on a pathway of:

Sexual immorality, impurity, debauchery, idolatry, witchcraft, hatred, discord, jealousy, rage, selfish ambition, factions, envy, drunkenness, and eventual loss of the kingdom of God.

The **way** of keeping in step with the Spirit will lead you on a pathway of:

Love, joy, patience, kindness, goodness, faithfulness, gentleness, and self-control.

Thomas' asked Jesus, "Lord, we don't know where you are going, so how can we know the **way.** Jesus answered, "I am the **way**, and the truth, and the life. No one comes to the Father except through me." (John 14:5 - 6) (If you have not already memorized John 14:6, work on memorizing it.)

Thomas, in his asking the question, was referring literally about the destination of the place Jesus was going to. He wanted to know a place, not a **way** of life. Jesus' answer pointed to Himself as the **way.**

How can Jesus be the **way?**

How are you walking in the **way** of Jesus, in the truth of Jesus and the life of Jesus? Give some examples. (Hint: Use the list of keeping in step with the Spirit. For example: I walk in the way of Jesus by being joyful even when life is difficult.)

In my teen years I participated in a boys ministry called Christian Service Brigade. Every meeting would end with us reciting the following benediction:

"Now we trust in God to make us bright and keen for Christ because we love Him and want to serve Him until we see Him face to face."

Often I use these words to remind myself that I need to remember to walk in the way of Jesus because of what He is cultivating in me through the Holy Spirit making me wiser as I serve His purpose and will.

Prayer: Using the words of that benediction, write your prayer of trust, love, and service as a **way** of life until you see Jesus face to face.

ABOVE ALL, "STAND FIRM"

"But thanks be to God! He gives us the victory through our Lord Jesus Christ. Therefore... **stand firm**. Let nothing move you. Always give yourselves fully to the work of the Lord..." 1Corinthians 15:57, 58a

What does it mean to "stand firm?" In the 1Corinthians passage above, Paul writes, "Let nothing move you." The image of standing firm is of a soldier who maintains a position, holds his ground, refusing to surrender or retreat. The assumption is that no threat will move that soldier. Paul uses that image to describe what it means to stand firm in faith. The writer of Hebrews wrote "Now faith is being sure of what we hope for and certain of what we do not see."(Hebrews 11:10) Because Jesus, through His resurrection, has won the victory over death for us, we can stand firm in our faith.

However, you cannot stand firm and then second guess or be double-minded. James writes in his letter to believers, "Consider it pure joy whenever you face trials of many kinds because you know that the testing of your faith develops perseverance." (James 1:2, 3) He goes on to say, "If any of you lacks wisdom, he should ask God, who gives generously to all without finding fault, and it will be given him. But when he asks, he must believe and not doubt." (1:5, 6a) In other words, standing firm is single-minded and uncompromising despite fear or anxiety. Standing firm chooses to single-mindedly focus on passing the test of your faith.

Refusing to change your mind under pressure is good advice for all kinds of situations in life. No one wants to be a coward or wishy washy. On the other hand, being stubborn just to get your way is the opposite of what it means to stand firm. One stands firm for truth and conviction.

"Now faith is being sure of what we hope for and certain of what we do not see." (Hebrews 11:10) Imagine you are standing on the free throw line at the end of an important basketball game. You have the opportunity to win the game if you make both foul shots. Under pressure, do you think, "I hope I make the shots?" Or worse yet, do you remember the failures of making foul shots under pressure in the past? Or do you stand firm being sure of what you hope for and certain of what you do not see? Which of these mindsets is likely to lead to winning the game?

Look back at how Paul challenges his readers to reflect on "the victory through our Lord Jesus Christ." In other words, the victory is already won, so "therefore stand firm." Do you believe in the gospel truth that by believing in Jesus you have eternal life? Focus on that truth daily and stand firm. Trials of many kinds will happen, but "let us hold unswervingly to the hope we profess, for He who promised is faithful." (Hebrews 10: 23)

Reflect: Where are you facing trials, doubts, fears, and/or anxiety that causes you to compromise your faith? Name them below.

Prayer: Pray the prayer below while you look at the list of trials, doubts, fears and anxieties.

Dear LORD, show me where in my life I am double-minded, hedging my bets, and compromising my convictions. I know that my fearfulness causes me to retreat instead of stand firm. I seek to be comfortable in my life instead of being single-minded in my faith in You and Your promise of eternal life. I want to be strong in faith today standing firm giving myself fully to Your work in me being sure of the victory through Jesus. Amen

Week 11, Day 2 Reflection

Essential 11: Above all else, "stand firm" 1Corinthians 15:57, 58a

"...be strong in the LORD and in His mighty power. Put on the full armor of God so that you can take your **stand** against the devil's schemes. For our struggle is not against flesh and blood, but against the rulers, against the authorities, against the powers of this dark world and against the spiritual forces of the heavenly realms. Therefore put on the full armor of God, so that when the day of evil comes, you may be able to **stand** your ground, and after you have done everything, to **stand**. Ephesians 6:10 - 13

Reread Ephesians 6:10 - 13 and answer the following questions:

Where does our strength come from to stand against the devil's schemes? (Ephesians 6:10)

Who are the enemies?

What is the purpose of the armor of God?

How are we to face the day of evil?

Prayer: Dear LORD, I desire to stand against evil spiritual forces by counting on your mighty power and your full armor. Amen

Week 11, Day 3 Reflection

Essential 11: Above all else, "stand firm" 1Corinthians 15:57, 58a

Read Ephesians 6:14 - 17 and complete each of the quotes below.

Paul writes "**stand firm then**" ...

"With the belt of _____"

"With the breastplate of _____"

"With your feet fitted with _____."

"Take up the shield of _____"

"Take the helmet of _____"

"And the sword of the _____ which is the _____."

Each of the armor parts equips us to stand firm against the attack of spiritual forces. From the fill in words above explain how each armor part helps us to "**stand**" our "ground" on "the day of evil."

Belt:

Breastplate:

Fitted feet:

Shield:

Helmet:

Sword

Prayer: Father God, equip me to stand firm against evil spiritual powers by Your gospel truth, righteousness, and protection, joined by my faith in Your salvation and Your word. Amen

Week 11, Day 4 Reflection

Essential 11: Above all else, "stand firm" 1Corinthians 15:57, 58a

Read: Ephesians 6:18a "And pray in the Spirit on all occasions with all kinds of prayers and requests."

Why does Paul conclude his armor of God illustration with this verse? Hint: Delete the first word and insert "Above all else," at the start of Ephesians 6:18.

Read: James 5:13a & 16b "Is any one of you in trouble? He should pray... [because] The prayer of a righteous man is powerful and effective."

Prayer is powerful and effective! Why?

Considering the specific issue of feeling challenged to stand firm in the face of an attack by spiritual forces, prayer takes on an increased urgency. When in your past did you cry out or strongly petition God because of the trouble you were facing? Do you remember the urgency and perhaps the panic you felt? Imagine in that moment you knew nothing about prayer and you had no belief or faith in a loving God. Would you be able to stand firm?

According to James, when you are powerless, prayer is powerful and effective, but prayer does not change God. Prayer empowers and changes you to be able to stand firm by reminding yourself that God is sovereign over all of creation and time. In other words, He is in control even when everything looks out of control. That is why James wrote "Consider it pure joy… whenever you face trials of many kinds…" (James 1:2) By praying first, you can consider the circumstances as an opportunity to stand firm in the testing of your faith by focusing on "God, who gives generously without finding fault." (James 1:5b) Single-minded prayer looks at God's power and sovereignty instead of the enemy. Take your eyes off the enemy and focus them on God.

Prayer: God is for you, not against you! Write a prayer asking God to change your fearful mindset into a thankful mindset "giving thanks in all circumstances for this is God's will for you in Christ Jesus." 1Thessalonians 5:17

Weak 11, Day 5 Reflection

Essential 11: Above all else, "stand firm" 1Corinthians 15:57, 58a

Do you know Nehemiah's story? Nehemiah lived in exile serving King Antaxerxes. When he had heard from those who survived the exile that the walls and gates of Jerusalem were broken down and burned, he sat down and wept, mourned, fasted and prayed this prayer:

> "O LORD, God of heaven, the great and awesome God, who keeps His covenant of love with those who love Him and obey His commands, let your ear be attentive and your eyes open to hear the prayer your servant is praying before you day and night for your servants, the people of Israel…" (Nehemiah 1:5 - 6)

Nehemiah follows that prayer with confessions naming how he and his fellow exiles had sinned against God. Then, calling on God to equip him to restore the walls and gates of Jerusalem. His prayers were so powerful and effective that King Antaxerxes allowed him to go and survey the damage and then create a plan for restoration of the walls and gates. However, there were enemies who schemed to kill Nehemiah and stop the rebuilding efforts.

Read Nehemiah 6 and put a check mark next to verse 3 and 11. How does Nehemiah demonstrate that he **above all else stands firm**?

> Verse 3

> Verse 11

What was the result of Nehemiah's standing firm in the face of the threats? See verses 15 - 16.

Prayer: Dear LORD, I confess my desire to avoid standing firm by choosing comfort and escape. I am often afraid that Your will for me is too hard. Help me to understand that You have already won the battle for me and your kingdom. Give me the courage to stand firm in times of trouble, and I will give you the glory. Amen

Week 11, Day 6 Reflection

Essential 11: Above all else, "stand firm" 1Corinthians 15:57, 58a

Anxiety and fear are the enemies of standing firm. The Apostle Peter writes at the end of his first letter the following instructions. "Cast all your anxiety on [God] because He cares for you. Be self-controlled and alert. Your enemy the devil prowls around like a roaring lion looking for someone to devour. Resist him, standing firm in the faith..." (1Peter 5:7 - 9a)

Quite an image! Because we live in neighborhoods free of prowling lions, we may miss the urgency of Peter's warning. (Actually, I think our striving for safety and easy living may make us even more vulnerable "against the powers of this dark world and the spiritual forces of the heavenly realms.") Perhaps the following story may help.

When we lived in Kenya, my son and I decided to explore Kenya's Aberdare National Park. We had heard that the Aberdare mountains rise up to 14,000 feet with majestic waterfalls, forest elephants, lions, and rare species. Because we arrived late in the afternoon, we decided to take a short drive to explore before sunset, planning on returning the next day for a full exploration. When we told the Ranger at the gate about our plan. He pointed us to a short loop to explore, but he warned us that the park closed at sunset. In our Nissan double cab pickup truck we slowly drove on the loop looking for wildlife. When we came to a rise, where at the top we noticed a wet and muddy area at the bottom of the hill, I shifted to four wheel drive, revved the gears and drove into the mud patch. Then I felt the truck slowly sink in the mud. Trying to impress my son, I put the truck into reverse to back out, but the truck sank even deeper. I shifted to first gear and the wheels just spun in place until they stopped because the mud had caked onto the tires. At that point I knew we were mired, but I acted like it was no problem. We got out to look at the predicament. I found a plastic milk gallon that had been cut to be a scoop in the truck. I used it to try to dig out the mud on the front and back of all the wheels, to no avail.

Because the Aberdares are on the Equator, night falls abruptly. Knowing that, we tried several more times revving the engine going forward and backward, but soon we realized we were stuck for the night. Then It began to rain. We got back into the truck and talked about our situation. The park was closing. We were about 3 miles away from the gate. Should we spend the night in the truck, or should we hike out to the gate?

We knew that at this elevation the temperature would drop to the low 40s. Furthermore we had no blanket and we were dressed in shorts and tee shirts. We also knew that we were in a game park full of elephants, cape buffaloes, and lions. Meanwhile, the rain continued and it became pitch black. We began to shiver in the cold truck cab.

That is when I decided that we were going to abandon the truck and follow the dirt road to seek help at the gate. My heart was in my throat, but I had to put on a brave show. We could smell the elephants and we imagined that any moment a lion would charge out of the thick growth on either side of the road. Praying constantly, I knew that I had made a foolish mistake, but by that time we were further from the truck than the gate. I have never felt so anxious and fearful in my life.

Obviously, we got to the gate without being devoured by lions. There is more to this story, but I will conclude by saying that after spending the night at the gate in a room of one single bed and one wool blanket, in the morning the Ranger with his rifle hiked with us to our truck. We discovered that the truck was encircled with elephant prints and dung. The Ranger told us to gather the dung and pack it under the wheels. The dung provided traction to get out of the mud.

While I am not proud of my foolish decision to put my son and me in peril, I tell this story because I know what it is like to actually cast all my anxiety and fear on God while under the very real threat from a "roaring lion."

Reflect:
What decisions have you made that put you and others in peril from spiritual lions prowling around you. Stand firm, be self-controlled, and be alert! And above all else, cast your anxieties on God.

What are your anxieties? List them below.

Prayer: I know that I am not the only foolish person who ignores the danger all around me. Likely, you too have made foolish decisions. Talk to God. He cares for you "and the God of all grace, who called you to His eternal glory in Christ...will Himself restore you and make you strong, firm, and steadfast. To Him be the power for ever and ever. Amen." (1Peter 5:10 - 11)

ABOVE ALL, "FIGHT THE GOOD FIGHT"

1 Timothy 1:18 - 19a

Read 1Timothy 1:18 - 19a. Then answer the following questions: What is a *good* fight? What would be a bad fight?

> "Timothy, my son, I give you this instruction in keeping with the prophecies once made about you, so that following them you may fight the **good fight**, holding on to faith and a good conscience…"

Good Fight:

Bad Fight:

Apparently when Timothy was younger he had been challenged to play an active role in spreading the gospel, and the Apostle Paul had adopted Timothy as a spiritual son. So, the verses above would be received by Timothy as encouraging words from a revered mentor. In just a few verses that follow, Paul writes his specific instructions for fighting the good fight.

Read 1Timothy 2:1 - 5 below, and underline the words that indicate how to fight the good fight.

> "I urge, then *first of all*, that requests, prayers, intercession and thanksgiving, be made for everyone - for kings and all those in authority, that we may live peaceful and quiet lives in all godliness and holiness. This is good, and pleases God our Savior, who wants all men to be saved and to come to a knowledge of the truth. For there is one God and one mediator between God and men, the man Christ Jesus…"

What is first of all?

What does praying for all those in authority have to do with fighting the good fight?

I am writing this in the middle of the 2024 race for electing a President. This week the Democratic Party is meeting in Chicago for their convention. Within that context how do Paul's words in 1Timothy 2:1 - 5 instruct me to fight the good fight?

Prayer: Do you pray for all those in authority, even those who are in a different party? Verse 8 in Timothy 2 "I want men everywhere to lift up holy hands in prayer, without anger or disputing." Can you do that? Pray for all those who are in authority in your community, in your state, and in the federal government.

Week 12, Day 2 Reflection

Essential 12: Above all, "Fight the Good Fight" 1Timothy 1:18 - 19a

In Paul's second letter to Timothy written from prison, he knew that this letter would probably be his last communication with his spiritual son. He sensed that he was at the end of his life. So he writes "...I am already being poured out like a drink offering and the time has come for my departure. I have fought the good fight, I have finished the race, I have kept the faith." (2Timothy 4:6 - 7)

His letter to Timothy is Paul's last words of instruction for his mentee. Let's dig into those instructions that define the good fight for Timothy in each of the 4 chapters of this final letter.

Read 2Timothy 1:7 What words in this verse describe the good fight?

Read 2Timothy 1:8 - 12 What is Paul's instruction?

Read 2Timothy 1:14 What is Paul's instruction?

Prayer: Using the answers above, ask God to apply those instructions to your life.

Week 12, Day 3 Reflection

Essential 12: Above all, "Fight the Good Fight" 1Timothy 1:18 - 19a

Read 2Timothy 2:1: What is Paul's instruction?

Read 2Timothy 2:3 - 7 Paul instructs Timothy to "endure hardship." What are the three examples for how to "endure hardship?"

1.

2.

3.

Prayer: First reflect on those examples. Then ask "the LORD to give you insight into all this."

Week 12, Day 4 Reflection

Essential 12: Above all, "Fight the Good Fight" 1Timothy 1:18 - 19a

Read the following verses in 2 Timothy and answer the questions and fill in the blanks.

2Timothy 2:8 "Remember Jesus Christ..." For whom are you fighting the good fight?

2Timothy 1:8 "So do not be ashamed to testify _____."

2Timothy 1:9 - 14 How many times is Christ Jesus repeated?

2Timothy 2:1 "You then, my son, be strong in the grace that is _____."

2Timothy 2:3 "Endure hardship with us like a good soldier of _____."

Above all, fight the good fight by representing Christ Jesus!

Prayer: Ask God to remind you that fighting the good fight is not about you. It's all about representing Christ Jesus and making Him first and foremost in your life.

Week 12, Day 4 Reflection

Essential 12: Above all, "Fight the Good Fight" 1Timothy 1:18 - 19a

Read 2Timothy 2:22 Flee what? What are you to pursue?

Read 2Timothy 2:23 "Don't have anything to do with foolish and stupid _____."

Read 2Timothy 2:24 As the LORD' servant avoid _____ , but instead be kind to everyone.

The good fight avoids "foolish and stupid" arguments that lead to quarrels because quarrels lead to bad fights that divide people and create factions.

Prayer: Our world is full of dissensions, opinions, anger, disputes and hatred. Ask the Holy Spirit to show you where you need to flee evil temptation to be right by proving others wrong instead of pursuing righteousness, faith, love, and peace.

Week 12, Day 5 Reflection

Essential 12: Above all, "Fight the Good Fight" 1Timothy 1:18 - 19a

Read 2Timothy 3:1 - 5 Does this paragraph accurately describe our "terrible times?" Why or why not?

Read 2Timothy 3:10 - 11 How did Paul model fighting the good fight?

Read: 2Timoty 3:14 Describe what you have learned about and have been convinced of?

Prayer: Ask God to give you purpose and faith for everyday living in "terrible times."

Week 12, Day 6 Reflection

Essential 12: Above all, "Fight the Good Fight" 1Timothy 1:18 - 19a

Read 2Timothy 4:6 - 8 What is in store for Paul and not only him but also all others who patiently wait for the day of Christ' coming?

Read 2Timothy 4:7 What are the three ways that Paul persevered?

- "I have _____

- "I have _____

- "I have _____

Prayer: Commit yourself to fighting the good fight for God's kingdom always with eternity in view.

ABOVE ALL, "FEAR THE LORD," BUT DO NOT BE AFRAID

Read the verses below;

Deuteronomy 10:12 "And now, O Israel, what does the LORD your God ask of you but to **fear** the LORD your God, to walk in all His ways. To love Him, to serve the LORD your God with all your heart and with all your soul."

Deuteronomy 31:12 -13 "Assemble the people - men, women and children, and the aliens living in your towns - so they can listen and learn to **fear** the LORD your God…

1Samuel 12:24 "But be sure to **fear** the LORD and serve Him faithfully with all your heart; consider what great things He has done for you."

Proverbs 1:7 "The **fear** of the LORD is the beginning of knowledge, but fools despise wisdom and discipline."

Psalm 128:1 "Blessed are all who **fear** the LORD, who walk in His ways."

> Revelation 14:7 "He [an Angel] said in a loud voice, '**Fear God and give Him glory...**'"

It is clear in each of these verses that to fear the LORD is **not the same as being afraid** of God. According to these verses, to fear the LORD is to be so in awe of God that you love Him, serve Him, and walk in His ways.

I remember when I as a young teen I became an avid fan of the New York Yankees. In fact, the Yankee second baseman, Bobby Richardson, went to my church. (I know this memory really dates me because I loved the 1960s Yankees with Roger Maris and Mickey Mantle. Well, full disclosure, I still am a Yankees fanatic, especially for Aaron Judge.) In particular, I still remember 60 plus years ago, watching Bobby Richardson (2B) and Tony Kubek (SS) play ping pong in the church basement. Their skills, reflexes and quickness thrilled me. Because I felt so blessed to have such a special personal experience with my baseball heroes, I wanted to tell others, and walk in their ways considering the great things they were doing on the baseball field and in World Series games.

Are you in awe of the LORD? Why? Why not?

Prayer: Confess that you easily worship and walk in the ways of your personal heroes, while you struggle to fear the LORD, revering Him above all else.

Week 13, Day 2 Reflection

Essential 13: Above all, fear the LORD, but do not be afraid.

Read Matthew 8:23 - 27 The disciples of Jesus had an up close relationship with the Messiah, yet they were often afraid. They were in the same boat when without warning a storm came up on the lake. The disciples panicked saying, "LORD save us! We're going to drown!" What did Jesus say to them?

In Matthew 8:27 Matthew records that the men were amazed [or in awe] and asked themselves, "What kind of man is this? Even the winds and the waves obey Him."

The disciples revealed, in the midst of the storm, that they knew Jesus as a "man" who was their leader, not the Messiah or Son of God? Why does Matthew (and also Mark 4:36 - 41 and Luke 8:22 - 25) record this brief story? What is the difference between the fear of the LORD and being afraid?

Name the fears that handicap you because you are focused on being afraid instead of being in awe of the LORD of the universe.

Prayer: Almighty God, Creator of everything, and my LORD and Savior, help me to cast my fears on you, and instead trust in you to work out your plan for me to glorify you. Amen

Week 13, Day 3 Reflection

Essential 13: Above all, fear the LORD, but do not be afraid.

Read Joshua 1:1 - 9

When the LORD handpicked Joshua to lead the Israelites into the Promised Land, He gave Joshua specific instructions. What were they?

Joshua 1:6 Be

Joshua 1:7a Be

Joshua 1:7b Be

Joshua 1:8 Do not

Joshua 1:9 Be

Joshua 1: 9 Do not

But the LORD did not just say how to be. He also gave promises about how to be strong and courageous. What were they? Finish the following quotes:

Joshua 1:5b As I was with Moses, so I will

Joshua 1:8b meditate on [the book of the Law], so that

Joshua 1:8b Then you

Joshua 1:9b for the LORD

Do you find it difficult to not be afraid? Why?

I am writing just after the August 2024 Paris Olympics. The US had many strong and courageous performances, but none were more impressive than Simone Biles. Three years previously in Japan, Simone dropped out of the competition citing fear of injuring herself. Yet at this Olympics she came back to form by dominating the competition. Obviously, she had worked at turning away from being afraid by being focused on her training instead of her fear of failure.

Joshua turned his focus away from his fears and instead he focused on his fear of the LORD who promised that the LORD his God will be with him wherever he goes.

Prayer: Look at Proverbs 3:5 - 6 "Trust in the LORD with all your heart, and lean not on your own understanding. In all your ways, acknowledge Him, and He will make your paths straight." Then pray this prayer: I turn my entire focus on trusting and fearing you LORD, no longer trying on my own to be strong and courageous. Instead I want all my thoughts and actions to reflect my awe of You, LORD. Amen

Week 13, Day 4 Reflection

Essential13: Above all, fear the LORD, but do not be afraid.

When David, too young to be a soldier in King Saul's army, was sent to the front lines by his father to bring food for his brothers, he witnessed an entire army afraid of Goliath, a giant of a man who came out daily cursing the Israelite army for being wusses. No one volunteered to go out and fight Goliath because they all were afraid and intimidated. So, David volunteered to go out and fight Goliath.

What was David's mindset that overcame any fear? Read 1Samuel 17:32 - 37

Now read 1Samuel 16:1 - 13 David is anointed by Samuel to be the next _____. How does this event affect David's confidence to face off with Goliath?

Because David was in awe of God's protection and plan for him, he was confident about defeating Goliath. You may think that if you were anointed to be the next President of the United States, you would not be afraid, too. However, consider God's promise to you through His grace - you are guaranteed eternal life!

Prayer: Because "God so loved" me, "that He gave His one and only Son," so that I can reject fear and believe in Him and "not perish but have eternal life." LORD, I want to live by this truth so that your life reflects plainly what you have done in my life has been done through You.

Week 13, Day 5 Reflection

Essential 13: Above all, fear the LORD, but do not be afraid.

Read Philippians 2:5 - 8 The Apostle Paul's beautiful poetry about Christ Jesus begins with: "Your attitude [as a believer] should be the same as that of Christ Jesus." (Philippians 2:5)

- Look at the attitudes cited in Philippians 2:6 - 8.
  - o Although He was God, He "made himself nothing taking the very nature as a servant." (Philippians 2:6,7)
  - o "He humbled Himself and became obedient to death, even death on a cross." (Philippians 2:8)

Read Philippians 2:12 - 14

- Look at the attitudes that follow "Therefore…"
  - o Christ-like obedience (Philippians 2:12)
  - o Continuing working "out your salvation with **fear** and trembling." (Philippians 2:12)
  - o Doing "everything without complaining or arguing…" (Philippians 2:14)

Because our Savior, Christ Jesus, humbled Himself and was obedient to death on a cross, we are to humble ourselves and work out our salvation with fear and trembling. What does it mean to work out your salvation with fear and trembling? (See verses 14 and 15 below)

- Doing "everything without complaining or arguing so that you may become blameless and pure children of God without fault in a crooked and depraved generation, in which you shine like stars in the universe…" (Philippians 2:14, 15)

Prayer: Father God, change my heart from being self-centered to unselfishly do everything without complaining or arguing, because I want to reflect your light like the stars reflect light. Amen

Week 13, Day 6 Reflection

Essential 13: Above all, fear the LORD, but do not be afraid.

There was a time in my life when I would wake up nightly from dire nightmares sometime around 2 a.m. In those dark hours of the morning, I would become overwhelmingly afraid because I knew I was going to die sometime in the future. I would not be able to go back to sleep as I contemplated the end of my life. The only comfort I could find came from my repeating to myself over and over that death was years away for me. Because I was afraid of what it meant to die and the fact that one day I would die, my nightmares continued night after night.

Read Matthew 26:36 - 46

In this passage Jesus is facing his imminent horrible death on a cross. He knew that the time had come for Him to die for the sins of the world. So he went to a place called Gethsemane to pray. Matthew writes in verse 38 that Jesus said " My soul is overwhelmed with sorrow to the point of death." In pain He prays, "My Father, if it is possible, may this cup be taken from me. Yet not as I will, but as You will." (Matthew 26:39) Through prayer Jesus was "working out His salvation with fear and trembling," but He was not afraid. Again in Matthew 26:42, Jesus prays "My Father, if it is not possible for this cup to be taken away unless I drink it, may Your will be done."

How does Jesus model working out His faith in these two prayers? (Hint: How does He end each prayer?)

In this passage the disciples are clueless about what was about to happen, even though He told His disciples that His "soul is overwhelmed with sorrow to the point of death." (Matthew 26:38) Twice Jesus found them asleep. These disciples were ignorant about what the coming days would bring, and when Christ was arrested, tortured and crucified they scattered, afraid for their lives.

Do you see the difference between Jesus and His disciples? Jesus prayed fearfully for God's will to be done, while His disciples were not prepared for "the hour...the Son of Man is betrayed." (Matthew 28:46)

When we focus on our will and our plans eventually in our "crooked and depraved" time we will be afraid and unprepared because we are not in charge of our lives. But, if we watch and pray for God's will, not our will, to be done, by working out our salvation with fear and trembling, we will be without fault in a broken world.

Prayer: Your will, not mine, dear LORD. Make me aware, Holy Spirit, of the evil of wanting to be autonomous by following my own desires and dreams. When I awaken afraid at night, I will repeat, "thy will, not mine," recognizing that my will is temporary and Your will is eternal. Amen

ABOVE ALL ELSE, "SEEK FIRST THE KINGDOM OF GOD"

There are a lot of things, desires and achievements we seek during our lifetime, but above all else, seek first your Father God's kingdom.

Read Matthew 6:25 - 34

Fill in:

"Therefore I tell you, do not _____ about your life."

"Who of you by worrying can _____?"

"So do not _____, saying. 'What shall we eat?' or 'What shall we

drink?' or What shall we wear?' For the pagans _____,

and your heavenly Father knows _____."

"But _____ His kingdom and His righteousness

and _____."

Think about a time when you worried about not having enough funds to make it to the end of the month. What did you do? Who did you go to? Early in my marriage my wife and I were running after things above our income using credit cards to quench our thirst for things we could not afford. The credit cards had become our god who gave us what we wanted. Have you been there?

Credit cards like all false gods promise immediate gratification and then they demand never ending payments that are a kind of slavery leading to a life of worrying. When I realized that, I searched for a way for extra compensation trying to solve the problem myself. So, I became a door to door salesman to supplement my income. However, I was miserable! I began to see everyone, including my friends, as potential customers. I would choose a neighborhood for going door to door ringing doorbells. But as I walked up to each door, I would turn around and walk away hating myself.

Finally, I realized that I was trying to be the savior for our finances and our way of living. My wife and I decided to cut up all our credit cards and set up a plan for paying off our debts. In that way we repented from being so caught up with seeking first things we wanted. Repentance by definition means turning away from wrong behavior. So we resolved to seek first the kingdom of God. We went to our LORD in prayer seeking and asking for wisdom.

Read Matthew 7:7-8 "Ask and it will be given to you; seek and you will find; knock and the door will be opened. For everyone [who seeks the kingdom of God and] asks receives; he who seeks finds, and to him who knocks, the door will be opened."

Matthew 7:7 - 8 describes a way of life, not a one time free get out of jail card!

Prayer: Dear heavenly Father, I want to align my priorities with your kingdom priorities. Thank you that you are not a severe God that demands my obedience and enslaves me instead of being merciful and forgiving. I don't have to worry because you as a good Father know what I need for flourishing. I want to run after your will, not run after all the worldly things, knowing that you will provide like any good father. Amen.

Week 14, Day 2 Reflection

Essential 14: Above all else, seek first the kingdom of God

We had two daughters in college and a son going into high school, when my wife and I felt called to serve at the Rift Valley Academy in Kijabe, Kenya. I was a high school English teacher and track and field coach. My wife was working as a teacher's aide. The decision to follow the calling required that we both retire from our public school jobs and pack up our belongings in a fourty foot container, rent our house and move to Kenya where I would receive a stipend one third of what I was making. My public school colleagues thought we were being foolish.

That was in the summer of 1995. Four years later our two daughters graduated from college and our son graduated from the Rift Valley Academy with an appointment to the Air Force Academy. Subsequently, we moved back to the USA and I started a fruitful 17 years of serving in a Christian PreK - 12 school retiring with no debt and eventually a new calling to care for our three adult children, their spouses and nine grandkids as well as serving on the Board of Directors of The Anvil Academy, writing two books and facilitating men's bible studies.

As I look back, I recognize that nothing of the above was our doing except seeking first the kingdom of God.

Are you motivated to learn more about what it means to seek the kingdom of God? Study the verses below and write what you learn from each passage.

2Chronicles 7:14

Psalm 34:1-12

Psalm 119:10

Jeremiah 29:12-13

Hebrews 11:6

Prayer: Use the words from the verses above to inform your prayer.

Week 14, Day 3 Reflection

Essential 14: Above all else, seek first the kingdom of God

Read Proverbs 8:12 & 17 "I, wisdom, dwell together with prudence; I possess knowledge and discretion...I love those who love me, and those who **seek** me find me."

Throughout the first nine chapters of Proverbs, wisdom is personified as Lady Wisdom. Proverbs 8 has Lady Wisdom calling out to all who are simple saying, "Listen, for I have worthy things to say..." (Proverbs 8:6a) In verse 12 she highlights three important traits of wisdom - prudence, knowledge and discretion.

> Prudence: The ability to discipline yourself by being cautious.

> Knowledge: Knowing something gained from experience and learning.

> Discretion: The quality of good judgment.

Read Proverbs 8:33 - 35 "Listen to my (Lady Wisdom's) instruction and be wise; do not ignore it. Blessed is the person who listens to me, watching daily at my doors, waiting at my doorway. For whoever finds me finds life and receives favor from the LORD."

How do these verses about wisdom reflect what it means to seek first the kingdom of God? Hint: Seeking first the kingdom of God includes seeking wisdom, cautiousness, knowledge and good judgment.

Prayer: Ask the Holy Spirit to show you where in your daily life do you need to increase your prudence, knowledge or discretion? Use the definitions above. Dear Holy Spirit…

Where do I lack the ability to discipline myself and be cautious?

What have I learned that I need to apply what You have been teaching me.

Show me where I am not showing good judgment.

Week 14, Day 4 Reflection

Essential 14: Above all else, seek first the kingdom of God

Where are you being unwise, careless, stubborn and lacking self-control? Use the answers to these questions to ask the LORD for wisdom in seeking first the kingdom of God daily.

Careless:

Stubborn:

Lacking Self-control:

Then each morning for the remaining 3 days of this week start each day praying about how you can be prudent, grow in knowledge, and make wise decisions.

Then each evening write a review of how you have sought the kingdom of God throughout the day. Make it fun by assigning stars up to five.

1 star - I completely forgot.
2 stars - Infrequently remembered.
3 stars - Remembered but mostly failed.
4 stars - Most of the time I practiced prudence, knowledge, and discretion.
5 stars - I made the most of the opportunities to seek first the kingdom of God.

Day 4 Morning Prayer

Day 4 Evening Review

Day 5 Morning Prayer

Day 5 Evening Review

Day 6 Morning Prayer

Day 6 Evening Review

ABOVE ALL ELSE, MTMOEO

"Be very careful, then, how you live - not as unwise but as wise, **making the most of every opportunity,** because the days are evil." Ephesians 5:15 - 16

As a middle school principal, I encountered the drama and awkwardness of 6th through 8th grade adolescents. Because middle school is an incubator of significant growth in size and maturity, middle school students need a tolerant and safe environment for making mistakes in judgment and self-control. During this unique time of life, middle school students begin to move away from dependence on parents and toward friendships making parenting complicated and emotional.

I found that an important part of my role was to be a parental counselor as parents dealt with their middle school student. Mostly, the scenario of meeting with a parent, began with a parent setting up an appointment with me to dispute an in-school disciplinary situation or to blame a teacher for something their child told them about. Often, they mirrored the emotions of their child when they met with me, making the meeting at first adversarial. I learned that as I listened to their grievances, I needed to be patiently empathetic. It often was not easy as I heard accusations and demands about how their son or daughter was unfairly being treated. While the majority of the accusations often came from an exaggerated perspective, their child was experiencing real struggles with friendships, relationships, or their studies.

These meetings with parents were always uncomfortable and upsetting for me, until I discovered Ephesians 5:15 - 16. Paul, writing to the Ephesian believers, encouraged them to live "by the light" by recognizing that what they were experiencing was not a dire problem but an opportunity to make the most of. Usually, I would counsel by pointing out that middle school keeps no damning files or records that will follow their child throughout their life because middle school is a safe place to mature and learn from mistakes and relational dramas. Raising preteens and teens requires the perspective that this time of life requires the MTMOEO attitude recognizing that the situation is an opportunity to learn how to be wise because the days are evil.

Do you remember when you were in middle school? Are you glad that there are no permanent records of that time of your life? What did you learn from your middle school days? Write your answer below:

What do you wish you had learned in middle school? Write your answer below:

At this point of your life, give an example of how you are learning how to live, not as unwise but as wise?

Prayer: Dear LORD, help me to wisely make the most of every opportunity to live for you. Show me a problem that offers the opportunity for change because it is unwise. Amen.

Week 15, Day 2 Reflection
Essential 15: Above all else, MTMOEO

When Paul writes "make the most of every opportunity," he is summing up major instructions about how to live wisely as children of God.

Read Ephesians 4:17 - 32, and as you read finish the quotes below.

Ephesians 4:17 "So I tell you this, and insist on it in the LORD, that you must

_____

_____

Ephesians 4:22-24 "You were taught, with regard to your

former way of life, to put off _____

which is being corrupted by its deceitful desires; to be

_____

and to put on the new self, created to be

_____

Ephesians 4:29 "Do not let any _____,

but only what is helpful for _____

Ephesians 4:31 "Get rid of all _____,

_____, and _____,

_____

and_____, along with every _____.

Ephesians 4:32 "Be _____,

_____ to one another,

_____ each other, just as in Christ

God _____

Before praying, review the fill in answers. Which instruction is a difficult challenge for you? In other words, what do you still need to "put off" or "get rid of" so that you can "be kind and compassionate to one another?"

Prayer: Ask God to continue to change you into being more Christ-like. Be specific about what needs to be "put off" and gotten "rid of."

Week 15, Day 3 Reflection

Essential 15: Above all else, MTMOEO

Continue to fill in the blanks for Ephesians 5:1 - 14

Ephesians 5:1-2 Be _____ of God,

therefore, as dearly loved children and live a life of

_____ just as _____

and gave _____

as fragrant offering and sacrifice to God.

Ephesians 5:3 But among you there must not be even a

hint of _____

_____, or of any kind of

_____ or of _____ "

Ephesians 5:4 Nor should there be _____,

_____ or _____.

Ephesians 5:8b - 9 Live as _____

(for the fruit of the light consists of in all _____,

_____ and _____.)

Ephesians 5:10 and find out _____.

Ephesians 5:11 Have nothing to do with the fruitless deeds

of _____, but rather expose them.

What action(s) do you need to focus on as an imitator of God?

Prayer: Ask God to reveal where you need to clean up your behaviors and live as a child of light.

Week 15, Day 4 Reflection

Essential 15: Above all else, MTMOEO

"Be wise in the way you act toward outsiders; **make the most of every opportunity**." Colossians 4:5

Who are the outsiders – non-believers - in your life?

Why should you be wise in the way you are toward them?

How does making the most of every opportunity fit with being wise in the way you act toward outsiders?

Are those "outsiders" influencing you, or are you influencing them? Another way to look at this question is to ask yourself: Do the "outsiders" in your life know about your faith in Jesus and your commitment to God?

Prayer: Dear Holy Spirit, show me how to be an influencer for your kingdom with the outsiders in my sphere of influence. Amen.

Week 15, Day 5 Reflection

Essential 15: Above all else, MTMOEO

When Paul writes "make the most of every opportunity," he is summing up major instructions about how to live as children of God. In his letter to the Colossian believers, his instructions are very specific.

Read Colossians 3:1 - 16 and finish the quotes below:

Colossians 3:1 - 2 ...set your hearts on _____,

where Christ is seated at the right hand of God. Set your

minds on _____, not

on_____.

Colossians 3:5 Put to death, therefore, whatever belongs

to your earthly nature: _____,

_____, _____,

_____ and _____

Colossians 3:8 ...you must rid yourselves of all such things

as these: _____, _____,

malice _____ and _____."

Colossians 3:12 Therefore, as God's chosen people, holy and

dearly loved, clothe yourselves with _____,

_____, _____,

_____ and _____.

Prayer: Translate Colossians 3:17 into a prayer asking God your Father to
reveal what is in your heart, mind, earthly nature, and on your lips so that

in whatever you do, whether in word or deed, you will do it in the name of the Lord Jesus.

Week 15, Day 6 Reflection
Essential 15: Above all else, MTMOEO

Read 2Peter 1:3 - 8

Growing in maturity is hard work! You will make mistakes, but if you "make every effort to add to your faith goodness; and to goodness, knowledge; and to knowledge, self-control; and to self-control, perseverance; and to perseverance, godliness, and to godliness, brotherly kindness, and to brotherly kindness, love, you will grow in maturity and godly wisdom. (1:5)

Read Colossians 3:17 & 23

In both these verses Paul emphasizes that "whatever you do" do it "in the name of the LORD Jesus" (3:17) and "whatever you do, work at it with all your heart, as working for the LORD..." (3:23)

Read Ephesians 5:15 - 16

Making the most of every opportunity is a lifelong process of carefully and prayerfully making every effort to whatever you do work at it with all your heart do it in the name of the LORD. Don't give up!

Prayer: Read 2Peter 1:5 again. Pray through the list of attributes and ask the Holy Spirit to reveal what you need to add to your awareness for the next steps of your growth as a follower of Jesus.

CONCLUSION

Congratulations, you have finished 15 weeks of devotions about 15 "above all" essential biblical themes for increasing your faith, knowledge and understanding of God's work in and through you for His kingdom and your flourishing.

If you are like me, you will need to remind myself that I am still learning and applying these 15 biblical essentials imperfectly. So, below are some suggestions for keeping these "above all" essentials in mind.

- Devote yourself to daily prayer and daily reading God's word. If you are consistent in this discipline, you will come across truths that jump out at you because of what you have learned in this devotional. "All scripture is God-breathed and is useful for teaching, rebuking, correcting and training in righteousness, so that the man of God may be thoroughly equipped for every good work." (2Timothy 3:16, 17)
- Review once a week one of the 15 Essential Above All devotions.
- Commit to taking 15 weeks annually to work through this devotional again.
- Consider asking a friend to work through this devotional with you. (I have found that I learn better when I share what I am learning.)
- Are you in a small group? Consider using this guide for your small group discussions.
- Remember who is "above all...The one who comes from heaven... Whoever believes in [Him] has eternal life." John 3:31, 32, 36

ADDENDUM A:
PRAYER JOURNAL

If somehow you recorded and saved your prayers, what would you discover? Try this week to daily journal your prayers by writing them down.

Day 1

Tonight just before you go to bed write in your prayer journal thanking God for something that happened today.

Day 2

Read Matthew 6:9 - 13:

> Our Father in heaven,
> hallowed be your name,
> your kingdom come,
> your will be done
> on earth as it is in heaven.
> Give us today our daily bread.
> Forgive us our debts
> as we also have forgiven our debtors.
> And lead us not into temptation,
> But deliver us from the evil one.

List the requests below.

"hallowed _____,

your _____,

your _____,

on _____."

Give _____.

Forgive _____, as

_____.

And _____,

but _____.

Who is the focus of the first sentence?

Who is the focus of the second sentence?

What is the condition cited in the third sentence? In other words, the request is conditional to what actions?

What is the compound request of the last sentence?

Prayer: In your prayer journal personalize your prayer following the order of the LORD"S Prayer. (Hint: Review the questions above.)

Day 3

Ephesians 3:14 - 21

"…I kneel before the Father, from whom his whole family in heaven and on earth derives its name. I pray that out of his glorious riches, he may strengthen you with power through his Spirit in your inner being so that Christ may dwell in your hearts through faith. And I pray that you, being rooted and established in love, may have power with all the saints, to grasp how wide and long and high and deep is the love of Christ, and to know this love that surpasses knowledge - that you may be filled to the measure of all the fullness of God.

"Now to him who is able to do immeasurably more than all we ask, or imagine, according to his power that is at work within us, to him be the glory in the church and in Christ Jesus throughout all generations, for ever and ever! Amen"

Prayer journal: Write a prayer (like the Ephesians 3:14 - 21 prayer) about someone(s) you care about.

Day 4

Use the Hillsong lyrics below from the song Hosanna to help you ask God to change you.

"Heal my heart, make it clean.

Open my eyes to the things unseen.

Show me how to love like you have loved me.

Break my heart for what breaks yours.

Everything I am for your Kingdom's cause,

As I walk earth to eternity."

Prayer journal: Write a prayer like the lyrics above asking God to change you. (Go ahead and use some of the same words but be more specific about what you want God to change in you.)

Day 5

Prayer journal: In your journal write a prayer about someone you know who needs daily prayer because of their deep needs or circumstances.

Day 6

Review your prayer journal, and then using what you have learned about prayer create an outline you can use for your daily prayer time. Write the outline down so that you can review it each day before your time of prayer.

Day 7

Record your prayer that follows your outline for daily prayer adding current needs and circumstances.

If you have found that the outline plus current additions is helpful, buy a journal and continue to write your prayers each day.

ACKNOWLEDGMENTS

I am grateful for the encouragements and advice I received from Fred Everett, Kimberly Neel, Michael Elwood, Darren Petersen and Peter Young.

This devotional project is inspired by four high school juniors – Connor Willis, Bray Holcomb, Mason Paige and Colt Muschara - who have met with me on Monday mornings before school to explore God's word. This devotional guide was written specifically with them in mind.

Above all else, I am thankful for my wife's patient spirit and love as I worked on this project the summer of 2024.

Printed in the USA
CPSIA information can be obtained
at www.ICGtesting.com
CBHW020202301124
18173CB00042B/418

9 798385 036585